THE LOOKOUT

❖

Cable Ships

National Maritime Museum, Greenwich

Society of Model Shipwrights Exhibition

Cable ships

Recently a reader mentioned that he had been intrigued to come across some notes about cable ships in a book just purchased. He described them as a 'most obscure variety of vessel'. It is true that they do not receive as much coverage as other ships. Which may be why they rarely feature as the subject for a model. Yet from the later part of the nineteenth century the technical journals have carried quite a number of detailed articles with arrangement plans. With their own and quite distinctive profile, these ships, and particularly some of the earlier vessels with their graceful, almost yacht-like appearances, could provide a subject for an interesting model.

National Maritime Museum, Greenwich

At the end of August 2002 the following press release was issued by the above museum.

Museums combine to form centre for display and storage of maritime models at historic dockyard, Chatham.

Initial plans are being finalised for a new Maritime Models Collection Centre to be opened on the site of the Historic Dockyard, Chatham, Kent, in 2006. The Collection Centre would house the reserve maritime model collections of the National Maritime Museum, Science Museum, and Imperial War Museum, as well as that of the Historic Dockyard.

The collections would be located in an open store facility which would be open to the public as an additional visitors attraction on the Chatham site. This will be supported by an introductory display, research facilities and closed storage for models awaiting conservation. The possibility of incorporating conservation facilities into the centre is being assessed. To complement the Centre itself, the four institutions will combine to set up on line access to the model collections on site and via their own websites.

The project is at an early stage, with the brief for a feasibility study currently underway. It is hoped that this study will be completed by the end of September 2002. Assuming approval of plans and securing of funding for the project, the collections could be installed in the No.1 Smithery building at Chatham during 2006, which currently attracts around 200,000 visitors a year.

Up to 5000 ship models will be housed in the Centre. These will date from the eighteenth to the twentieth centuries and include both naval and merchant shipping. Models of dock-

The twin-screw cable ship *Viking*, built in 1901 by Armstrong, Whitworth & Co. Ltd, Newcastle upon Tyne.

Photograph from the Editor's collection.

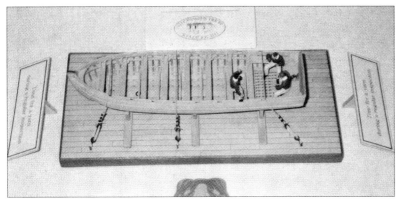

Ship's longboat (1800–1850) by Pat Earle. Scale 1:48.

yards, engines and other maritime subjects will also be included.

The collaboration is an example of the work of the United Kingdom Maritime Collections Strategy (UKMCS), founded in 1998 to explore ways in which maritime institutions could work together for the future collection, presentation and marketing of UK maritime heritage. UKMCS plans include co-operation aiming museums to share information and digital images of the nation's maritime collection, further long- and short-term loans and other partnerships between the UK maritime museums and the sharing of maritime expertise. The UK maritime collection numbers some four million objects over 50 per cent of which are currently housed in the National Maritime Museum and its outstations.

Statement (from Historic Dockyard): 'The new Centre is a great example of the kind of partnership between maritime museums which the UKMCS was formed to provoke. Although working primarily as a collections storage centre, it would also offer exhibitions and displays for the visitors to the site and an opportunity to view some of the finest examples of maritime models in existence.'

The first point to note about this proposed project is that it is directed at museums' reserve collections. Museums have always had such collections, albeit some have increased markedly in recent years as the num-

bers of models on public display have been considerably reduced. Although this is an initial announcement, questions immediately arise. What proportion of these reserve collections will be on open display, and what form will this take? Will the ship model be accorded its rightful place in the history and development of the ship, without becoming a mere adjunct to a 'theme'? Will there be adequate facilities for researchers and research work? What does that reference to 'marketing' foretell? The NMM statement refers to 'open display'. That of the Dockyard to the 'opportunity to view selected models'. Could this mean a show within a show, or something else?

We will include further information about the project as it is made available. In the meantime we would be interested in readers' views based on the content of this initial announcement. These could include any on the choice of location and its accessibility – a point which we have for the moment, excluded from our first reactions pending hearing readers' thoughts on it.

Society of Model Shipwrights Exhibition

The Society's Biennial Exhibition was held last October. The show comprised over a hundred models, and visitors were able to see models of a very wide range of ship types, ancient and modern, warships and merchant vessels, working and static. The exhibits ranged from miniatures at 1:600 scale through to 1:12 scale working models both steam and sail. There were also a number of fine marine paintings. During the course of the exhibition a number of the Society's members gave demonstrations of the art and craft of ship modelling techniques, ranging from hull construction to rope making and lathe work. [*We are grateful to SMS member Clive Nightingale for these notes and photographs. Ed*]

Demonstration of making wooden ship hulls by Peter Heriz-Smith. A skin of brown sticky paper, formed on a mould, when released can be planked with strips of wood.

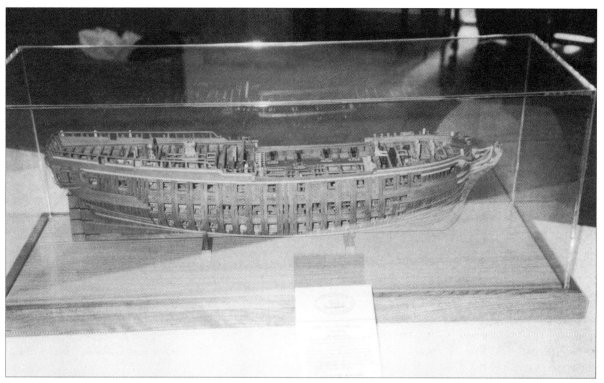

28-gun frigate *Triton*, of the *Mermaid* Class, by Keith Smith. Scale 1:64.

HMS *Malabar* (1818), built of teak in Bombay, and not broken up until 1905. Model by Ian Stranack.

HMS *Bulldog* (1968) by George LeRoche. Scale 1:48.

38-gun frigate HMS *Diana* (1794) by Bernard Fountain. Scale 1:48.

Corbita – a typical Mediterranean merchant vessel circa 300AD, by John Carter. Scale 1:32.

SS *Kakariki(1926)*, Union SS company of New Zealand coaster. Model by Arthur Sheldon. Scale 1:64.

Armed launch (1903) by Dennis Surridge.

Yacht *Yankee* (1925) by Douglas Rose. Scale 1:12.

Henrietta, Royal Yacht of 1679

An Admiralty-style model

by Gilbert McArdle, MD

The *Henrietta* was originally constructed for the personal use of Charles II (1660–1685) in 1679 and named after his mother. The ship model of the *Henrietta*, constructed in the same year, resided in England for many years until its purchase in the early 1930s by Colonel Henry Rogers, an associate of John D Rockefeller. It was recently on display with the Rogers's Collection at the USA Naval Museum in Annapolis, Maryland, USA.

Charles II is regarded by many to be the 'father' of the grand sport of yachting, and was somewhat of a profligate (among others) in his sponsorship of the construction of royal yachts, the *Henrietta* being the last of a total of 26. He apparently cultivated a love of 'yachts' during his sojourn as an exile in Holland before his restoration. In fact, the word 'yacht' is derived from the Dutch (to quote from Peter Kemp's *Oxford Companion to Ships and the Sea*) it is the pp of *jachten*, to hurry, to hunt, and it first appeared in the English language in 1660, the year of the restoration of Charles II, and the presentation to him by the State General of Holland of the *Nary*, a private pleasure vessel.

The *Henrietta* was not strictly used by Charles as a pleasure vessel, but was employed in other duties such as a dispatch vessel and scout, particularly in the Battle of Bantry Bay in 1688. Charles II's son, the Duke of York, later to be crowned James II, was probably a better sailor than his father, but his royal zeal for sailing was severely thwarted by his share in the debacle at the Boyne, and his subsequent exile to France.

For many years before and after the purchase of the model by the American collector, Colonel Henry Rogers, it was thought to be a replica of the Stuart Royal Yacht *Mary* of 1673. Recent copious evidence unearthed, including that by Major Grant Walker, the curator of the Roger's Collection at the US Naval Academy, has clearly demonstrated that the model is in reality that of the *Henrietta*. Regardless of name, the model was constructed in the typical and beautiful admiralty or English dockyard style of the late seventeenth century by an adroit modeler in the scale of ⅜in = 1ft in boxwood and some type of fruit wood, my guess being apple.

The keel length of the *Henrietta* was 65ft 0in, with a beam of 21ft 8in. The original model was rigged (not usual for such models as the Admiralty's rigging establishments were well codified by that date), but it was re-rigged in the 1930s by Henry Culver at the behest of Col. Rogers. Although Culver had exquisite skill as a modeler, there have been questions posed as to the historical authenticity of the re-rig of the *Henrietta*. I chose therefore to avoid controversy and did not rig the model. The resultant increased portability additionally lessened the tug at my conscience.

The draughts for the *Henrietta* were obtained from enlargements of the originals drawn by Daniel Parisier after lines taken off the

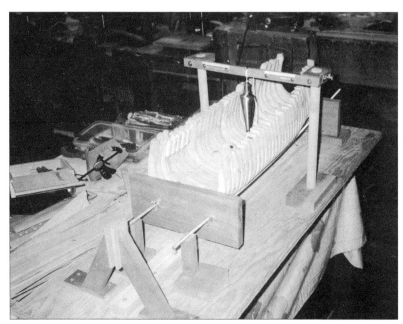

1. Hull frames mounted in jig.

Figure I. Draughts of the *Henrietta* by Daniel Parisier,
courtesy of Nautical Research Journal.

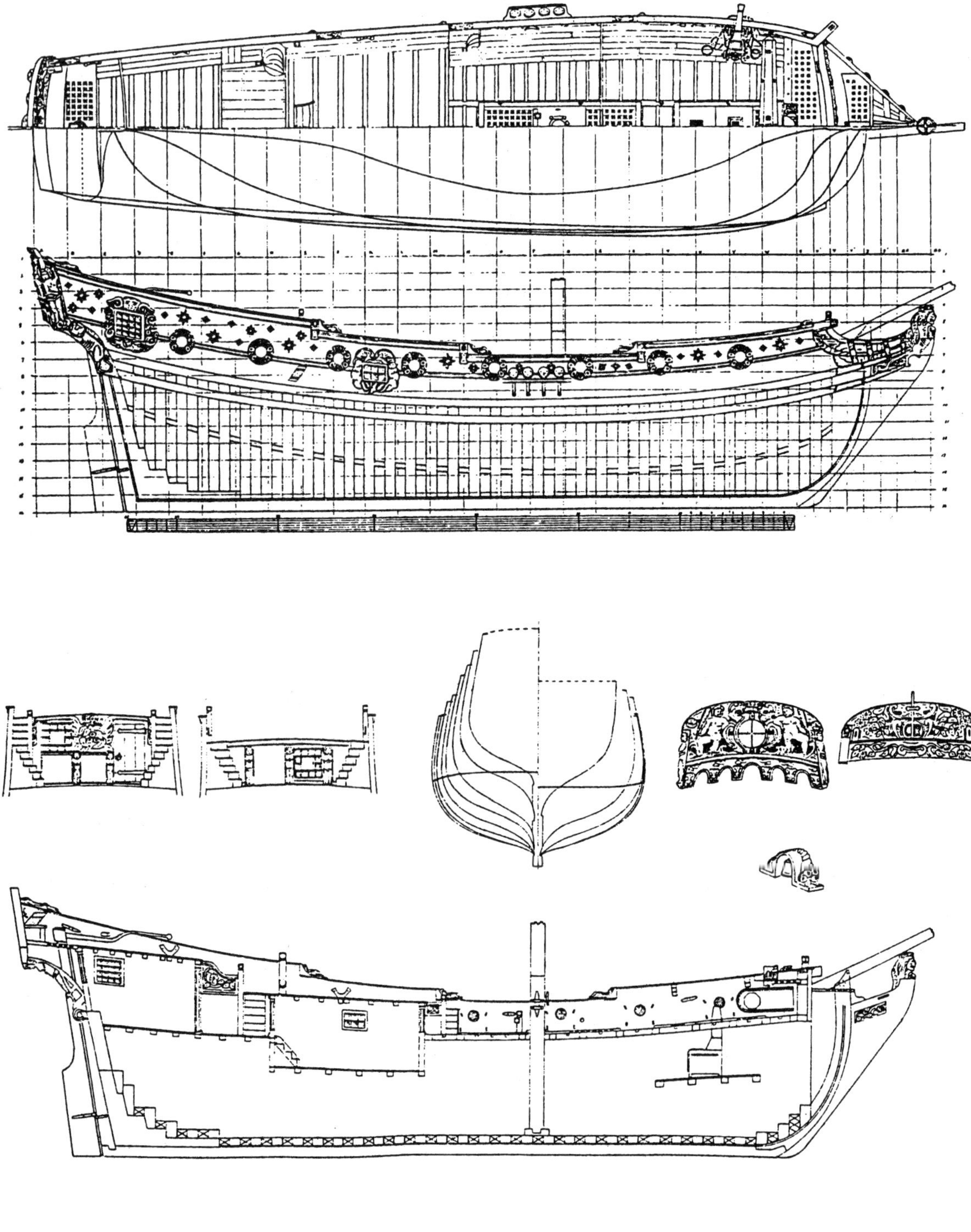

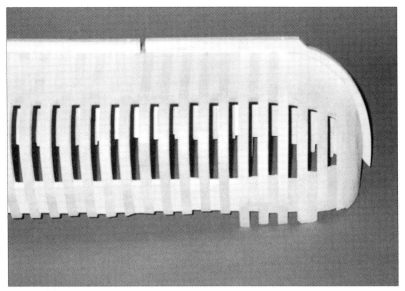

2. Bow frames.

original model. Mr Parisier had these draughts published in an article in the *Nautical Research Journal* entitled 'Taking Lines Off an Existing Model: Medium Research Technique' (*NRJ* Vol 40: 128–31, 1995). Major Grant Walker also kindly allowed me to photograph and take additional pertinent measurements from the *Henrietta*. Mr Parisier's draughts are reasonably accurate, the only minor corrections being making all of the transverse bow timbers lie at right angles to the water line, and revising a miscalculation in the amount of tumblehome.

Hull construction

As with other admiralty models that I have constructed, I prefer to build the model in an upright position (in contrast to the upside down method popularized by Harold Hahn, and use a jig initially described by Harold Bruckshaw in *Ships and Scales* in 1985. With this jig, the keel may be kept rigidly in place, while the frames are added. ensuring with the overhead plumb-bob that the mid-line of these frames is accurately and progressively maintained as noted in Photograph 1.

The keel was fashioned from ⁵⁄₁₆in thick English boxwood. The frames

were made from Brazilian boxwood (obtained from Canada). In recent years I have employed Brazilian and Maricaibo (Burma) boxwood due to the extreme difficulty in obtaining European or English boxwood (*buxus sempervirens*) in the USA. Brazilian boxwood is straighter grained but more beige in color and lacking the crisp yellow appearance of English box. The frame construc-

tion in the seventeenth century was considerably less complicated than multiple futtocked frame construction of the eighteenth century, as shown in the drawing of Figure 1.

I began by tracing the shape of each frame and interpolated frame from the body plan on tracing paper. These outlines were then transferred to the boxwood ready for cutting out each frame with a bandsaw. I should mention, perhaps controversially, that I make no attempt to cut the appropriate taper on each frame, feeling that the subtle and forever altering variation in frame fore-and-aft shape is impossible to constantly recreate on a bandsaw. Therefore I cut each from ¹⁄₃₂in to ⅛in greater in outboard and inboard dimension before gluing the frames together (as everyone knows, there is always a degree of slippage when gluing and clamping frames together, particularly with white or yellow glue). After the frames are all glued together, I fair them to match a template derived from the body plan. I fair the outer hull with rasps and files and the inboard profile with files and Dremel power rasps. This method obviates attempting to fair

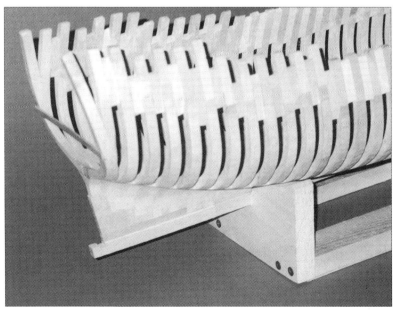

3. Stern frames.

4. Orlop deck beams, name plate, and mast step.

the frames before they are glued together. As most modelers soon realize, the hull has to be faired whether or not the frames have been taper cut initially, so why not save time and only carve them once?

When the outboard edges of the frames have been faired or carved to templated shape, the inboard portions of the frames are cut down with the usual dimensions of ⅛in to ³⁄₁₆in at upper level, ¼in mid frame and ⁵⁄₁₆in at the foot of the frame atop the keel. The floor frames were not morticed into the keel but alternately attached to the keel with dowel or small threaded brass screws in addition to white glue. It should be noted that the thickness of the frames (and the basswood chocks employed between the upper frames) were ¹⁄₆₄in less than ⅜in in thickness. It is very important, in my opinion, to cut all the strips of wood, which are going to be used for making the frames and chocks, at the same time in order to maintain uniformity of thickness, acknowledging the caveat that any slight variation in thickness of frames will progressively and arithmetically increase the error in the final scale length of the model (and its attendant frustrations), also keeping in mind that white glue applied at ⅜in intervals will increase the length of the model by approximately ³⁄₃₂in per 3ft of model regardless of the method employed to clamp or compress together each glued frame. Anyone who has employed a table saw for any length of time knows that it is extremely difficult to reset the saw's fence to match the exact thickness of a previously cut strip of wood; it is therefore advisable to error on the side of cutting too many strips for making

frames than too less. It should also be noted that the stempieces and deadwood are made from English boxwood in an attempt to increase the contrast between the beige of the Brazilian boxwood frames and the yellow of the deadwood and cutwater. The clean attachment of the stern frames to the deadwood is one of the most difficult processes in joinery of the entire model because each frame and its neighbor must be morticed very accurately into the thickest segment of the deadwood. I prefer to roughly cut out the mortices under size and then file each one to match the frame to which it will be attached, although if a good milling machine is available this slower and more painstaking method could be avoided. A boxwood stempiece was fashioned with a small section cut out for the stem carving and the small oblong hole for the bowsprit gammoning.

Wales

After the hull has been faired internally and externally and thoroughly sanded to 400 grit (aluminum oxide), the major wales were constructed of ¼in x ³⁄₁₆in American beech wood. In spite of its innate hardness, beech is very compressible and can

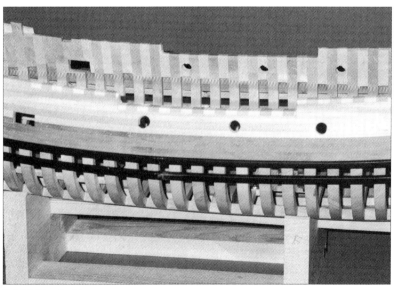

5. Midship planking.

readily be bent with steam or heat. I prefer to bend the strips of beech over the flat surface of a soldering iron. It is relatively easy to obtain any bend thus required with minimal effort. Any minor scorch marks on the inside surface may be readily scraped or sanded off. As my workshop is located in a basement furnace room where extreme variations in humidity occur (very humid in summer and very dry in winter), I experience horrendous problems with wood warpage and splitting. I have obviated some of this problem by making expansion joints in the major wales in an attempt to keep them from splitting off the model as the frames take on moisture, even when treenailed to every frame. After the outer edges of the wales have been gently rounded, this expansion joint is made of small strips of brass shims epoxied to the inner edge of one end of the beech wale and then wrapped about the joint before attaching the wale to the model. The wale is then painted flat (matt) black, drilled fore and aft so that it may be brass screwed on to the tapered frames, glued in place, and then double treenailed to each frame with #69 box or bamboo treenails. The exposed ends of the trimmed treenails are then cut off, sanded flat to the surface of the wale, after which the outer edge of the wale is repainted flat black, avoiding having to paint the previously painted superior and inferior edges of the wale where a clean black/beige edge with the frames is thus preserved.

Keelson, nameplate, breasthooks, and mast step

After attaching the major wales which considerably stabilize the conjoined frames, the keelson was fashioned of ³⁄₁₆in Kellow box and set in place with white glue and alternate frame attachment with ³⁄₆₄in dowels and small, straight-threaded brass bolts. Breast and stern hooks were made of ⁵⁄₁₆in boxwood as positioned over the keelson. The orlop or sta-

6. Upper stern planking encasing stern windows.

tionary deck beams were cut out with an appropriate camber (usually ¼in per foot of the breadth of the hull) from ⁵⁄₁₆in x ¼in Brazilian boxwood and glued in place as noted in Photograph 4. On two of these frames I mounted a small brass nameplate with small ornate brass screws. For many years I have renewed my somewhat narcissistic fetish of placing a nameplate in the bowels of the model incorporating the name and date of the vessel and my name. The mast step was fashioned from ⁵⁄₈in thick boxwood and glued in place. The nameplate and mast step are also noted in Photograph 4. The deck clamp for the deck floor for the midships cabin were made from ⅛in x ³⁄₁₆in beech, notched to receive the ends of the deck beams and glued in place.

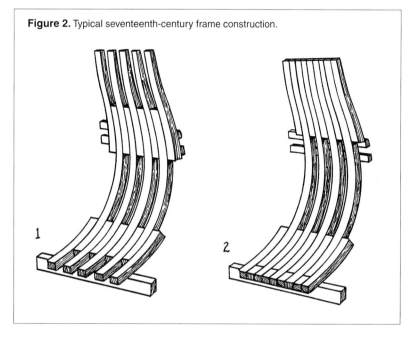

Figure 2. Typical seventeenth-century frame construction.

Planking

The outboard planking was commenced. The bottom half was made from $\frac{1}{16}$in x $\frac{3}{16}$/in and $\frac{1}{4}$in apple, and the upper half of similarly dimensioned beech. After being glued in place each plank was double treenailed per frame with #69 boxwood treenails. Box was used in place of apple or beech to maintain a contrast in wood colors, and to ensure that the treenails could be visualized. The gunports were drilled out to $\frac{3}{8}$in diameter, and the fore-and-aft window openings were cut out and fitted with upper and lower sills of $\frac{1}{8}$in x $\frac{1}{4}$in boxwood. A partial view of the planking and gun ports are as noted in Photograph 5.

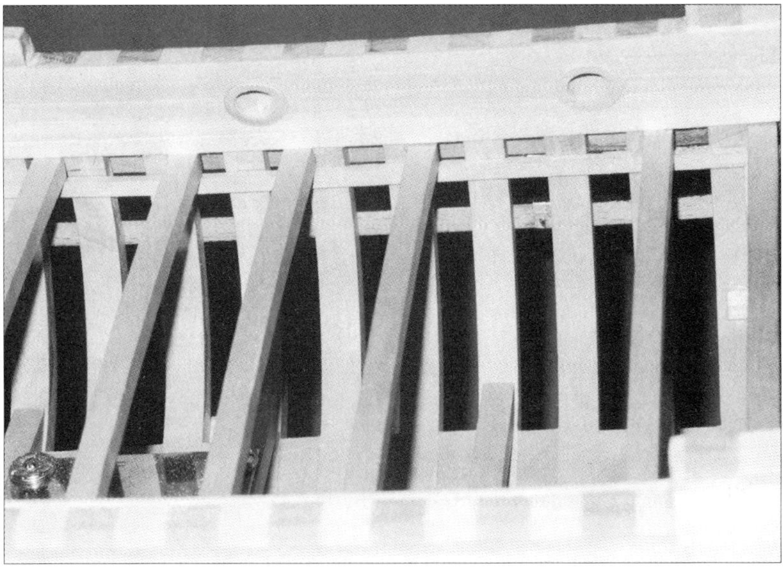

7. **Main deck beams with inboard planking.**

Stern

The stern planking was made from $\frac{1}{16}$in x $\frac{3}{16}$in apple and bent with a hot soldering iron to match the camber of the deck. The gunports were made of apple and fitted with brass hinges and ring bolts. The partially black painted sternpost ($\frac{5}{16}$in thick) was then glued in place. The stern windows were made from $\frac{1}{32}$in x $\frac{1}{16}$in boxwood. After completion, these windows were inserted into an applewood planking frame which was prefabricated as noted in Photograph 6, and painted with sky blue before being glued in place.

Deck beams

The deck beams were cut out (none steamed) with the standard camber to cross-sectional dimensions of $\frac{1}{4}$in x $\frac{3}{16}$in. These beams were glued in place on to morticed $\frac{3}{32}$in x $\frac{1}{4}$in main deck clamps as noted in Photograph 7. The $\frac{3}{64}$in x $\frac{3}{16}$in beech inboard planking, along with gunport collars, are also to be seen in this photograph. The carlings were made from $\frac{1}{4}$in x $\frac{3}{16}$in boxwood: the $\frac{1}{32}$in tenons at the ends of several of the carling pieces were cut on a small angled saw jig. Four rows of these carlings glued in place are shown in Photograph 8. The small mortices cut out for the $\frac{1}{16}$in x $\frac{3}{16}$in ledges are also visible in this Photograph, along with a small section of the partially decked orlop deck with $\frac{1}{32}$in x $\frac{3}{16}$in double treenailed holly strips. A drawing, Figure 3, demonstrates the placement and morticing of carlings.

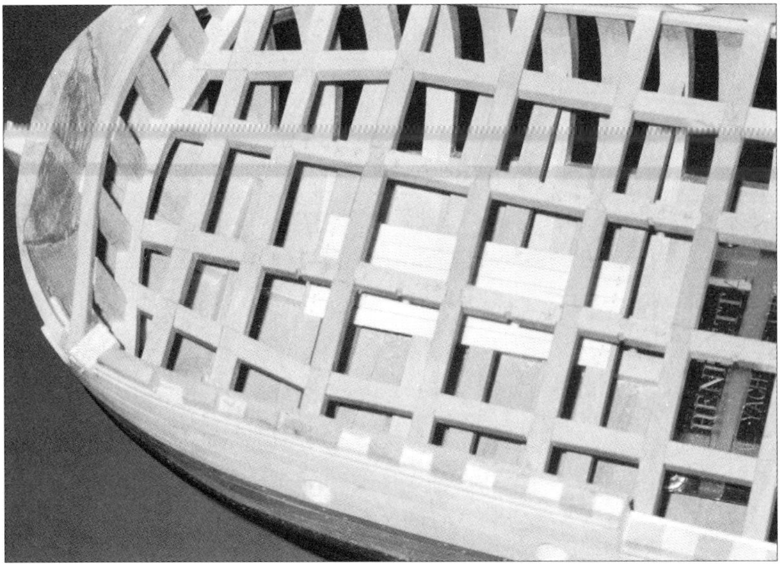

8. **Carlings in place.**

Decks

The quarterdeck cabin had a high ceiling and was entered though a door in the aft bulkhead to this cabin which was situated on a small separate deck between this bulkhead and the forward bulkhead for the poop cabin. Two stairwells led to this companionway from the aft sides of the quarterdeck. The lower segments of these two bulkheads were constructed of $\frac{3}{64}$in x $\frac{3}{16}$in basswood. The three completed bulkheads or partitions of the quarterdeck, aft quarterdeck, and poop deck are as noted in Photographs 9, 10 and 11 including windows, pearwood carvings, and brass-hinged doors. The

quarterdeck and poop beams were all fashioned from cambered boxwood ⅛in x ³⁄₁₆in. All the decks were partially planked with ½in x ³⁄₁₆in holly strip (to represent holystoned yellow pine or deck planks of other woods) with their edges pencilled to simulate tar (caulking) and double treenailed to each beam with #69 bamboo treenails (once again employing wood of a slightly different color to indicate the location of the treenails).

Fittings

The windlass was constructed of Swiss pearwood and its support timbers were made from beech. The galley was made of basswood with a base of the same material. Small pieces of cherry represented bricks, with thin strips of holly to represent mortar. The somewhat unusual staggered boxwood stairwells leading to the deck aft of the quarterdeck are as noted in Figure 1. The carved and gilt pearwood poop rails with black banisters were completed along with the attendant boxwood stanchions. The hatches were made from ⅛in x ³⁄₃₂in yellow boxwood notched on a jig somewhat similar to that described some years ago by Nepean Longridge in his book on the construction of HMS *Victory*, but modified and improved by Joseph McCleary by utilizing a double fence to prevent lateral movement of the boxwood while making the multiple notches necessary to mortice the hatches. The quarterdeck bulkhead and the small adjoining quarterdeck staircase can be seen in Photograph 12. The small carved ladies are noted in this Photograph: the first several pairs were carved from Swiss pearwood, but in the interest of time the remainder were white resin cast from RTV rubber molds made from the pearwood originals. The gild rails throughout the model were fashioned from Brazilian boxwood that was scored or scraped with a custom cut old X-acto blade, ground to the molding shape desired.

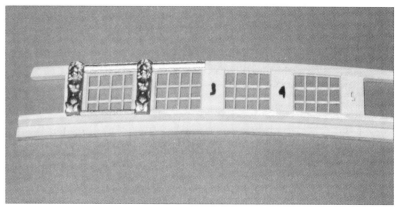

9. Quarterdeck bulkhead.

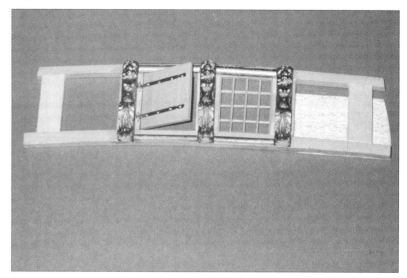

10. Aft quarterdeck bulkhead.

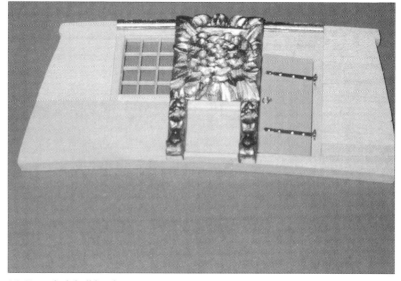

11. Poop deck bulkhead.

Bow

The bow lion was carved from pearwood. For ease of carving and handling, I mounted this on a piece of basswood cut to match the thickness of the stempiece on which the lion was to be mounted. When the lion had been carved, I cut out the mortice in the much softer basswood, and after gilding the lion, attached it to the stempiece, the top segment of which has already been painted flat black. The beakhead was constructed of beech. The progressive stages in the completion of the bow, including cheek pieces, rails, beakhead carvings, transverse bow timbers, together with the added carved ladies, cathead (made from ⅜in square boxwood, ¼in long and fitted with double brass sheaved), position of the fore hatches, windlass, carved belfry, and gammoned bowsprit stump, are as shown in Photograph 14.

Stern

The stern or transom boarding was carved out of cypress wood and then painted with gold paint. The somewhat complicated construction of the suspended stern is as in Photograph 14.

Because of the very intense detail-

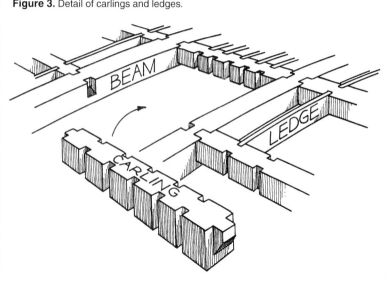

Figure 3. Detail of carlings and ledges.

ing in the coat of arms of Charles II, I was unable to carve this from wood. Instead I used a piece of incised sculpy, a clay-like sculptor's material that when briefly heated in an oven becomes very hard, and can be carved or sanded, etc. I made an impressed or female mold of the coat of arms with this sculpy and then, with a surrounding moat of sculpy, I poured white resin into this mold, and thus obtained the male or positive coat of arms. This was subse-

quently mounted in a hole drilled in the centre of the carved transom piece.

Fittings

The levers for the windlass were made from Swiss pearwood and mounted on black painted boxwood brackets. The carved poop seat, along with the carved hippopotami railing pieces, and main sheet sheave blocks, were completed and glued in place.

The rudder was positioned with two pairs of brass pintles and gudgeons. The carved boxwood tiller, after receiving a coat of flat black paint, was inserted into the mortice cut into the rudder stock and glued in place. The after flag mast was centrally positioned and held with a brass nailed support.

The two types of gun wreaths can be seen in Photograph 16. The prototypes were cut from boxwood, the remainder were white resin cast from RTV rubber molds obtained from the originals. Six carved cherubs were stationed at the break of the forecastle, quarterdeck, and poop deck.

The gunwale or sheer plank was made from 1⁄16in x ½in beech, painted black and secured in place with

12. Quarterdeck bulkhead and stairs.

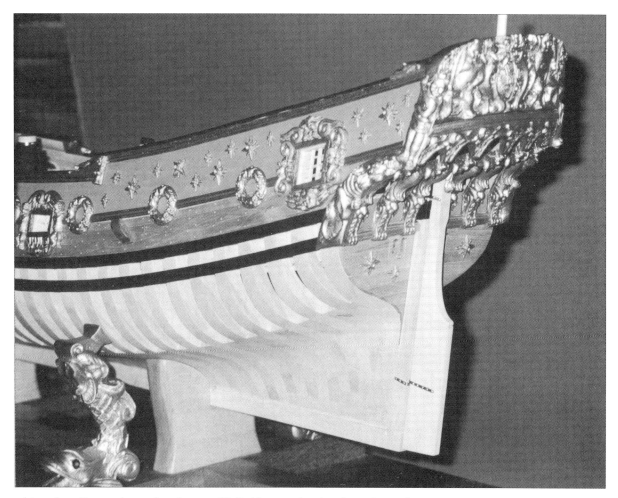

13. Rudder, stern framing, decorative work.

white glue. Forward on the sheer plank were two brass sheaved anchor fairleads with a trailing edge depicting a lion's paw. These were painted black and glued in place directly aft of the catheads.

Carved boxwood stars served as the prototypes for making RTV rubber molds for producing resin cast stars which were painted gold before being positioned on the sky blue painted upper planking.

The mast was made from ⁵⁄₁₆in maple and along with its four attached boxwood cleats was painted black before positioning though the turned boxwood main deck mastring and having its tenon inserted into the mortice of the mast step. The gun carriages and cannon visible in this photograph were made in the usual manner for the seven-

14. Completed top view of forecastle, including belfry, etc.

15. Completed stern.

teenth century. The carriages were made from pearwood, and the cannon were turned from maple and painted black. The gun carriages are almost identical to those of the eighteenth century except that the sides of the carriages are parallel and not tapered forward. The gun tackles were standard except for the large breech rope which was made utilizing a cut splice at its casabel attachment.

The anchor, as seen in Photograph 19 of the bow, was constructed in the usual manner with double boxwood brass strapped stock and a carved and black painted anchor. The buoy cable was double tied to the shaft of the angle and clove-hitched to its base before leading to the rigged, egg-shape boxwood anchor buoy in front of the mast channel, and then made fast to a forecastle kevel. The anchor was catted via a pearwood double brass sheaved and stropped block (½in x ⅜in), the rope being rove through the

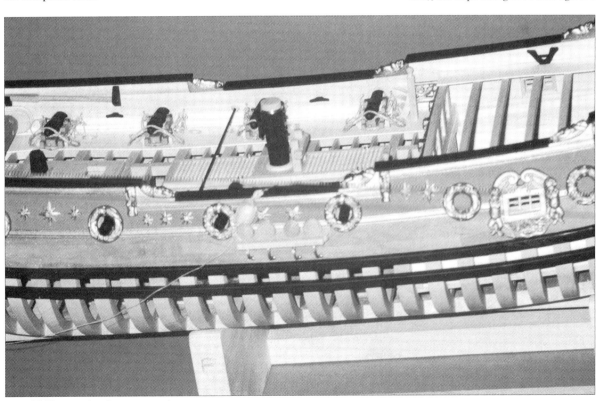

16. Midship area showing gun wreaths.

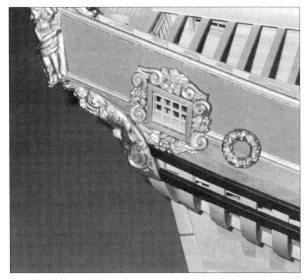

17. Aft cabin window carvings.

18. Cast and gold painted dolphin.

block and the cathead sheaves before being made fast to a forecastle cleat.

The deadeyes were turned from pearwood (⅜in x ³⁄₁₆in) and mounted though holes in the channels with annealed brass rings strops which in turn were attached to simple brass plates, typical of the seventeenth century (no chains were used). The carvings encircling the after cabin window of the *Henrietta* can be seen in Photograph 17.

Mounting the model

The model, supported by four carved dolphins, typical of the presentation of seventeenth century admiralty models, was mounted on a mahogany base board. A pearwood carved prototype dolphin served as an original for its cast counterpart. One of these dolphins with added ebony and bloodwood eyes may be seen in Photograph 18. The model is displayed in a case of black walnut with a bird's eye maple base, see Photograph 21.

Bibliography

David Parisier, 'Taking Lines of an Existing Model – a Medium Tech Solution', *Nautical Research Journal* Vol. 40, 128–131.

Bruckshaw, Robert, HMS *Royal Sovereign* (1787), *Ships in Scale*, Seaways Publishing, Inc., San Jose, California, July/August 1986.

Longridge, C Nepea, *The Anatomy of Nelson's Ships*, Model and Allied Publications, 1955.

Goodwin, Peter, *Construction and Fitting of the English Man of War 1650–1850*, Conway Maritime Press, London, 1987.

Lavery, Brian, *The Arming and Fitting of English Ships of War 1600–1815*, Conway Maritime Press, London, 1989.

Kemp, Peter (ed.), *The Oxford Companion to Ships and the Sea*, Oxford University Press, London, 1971.   ❏

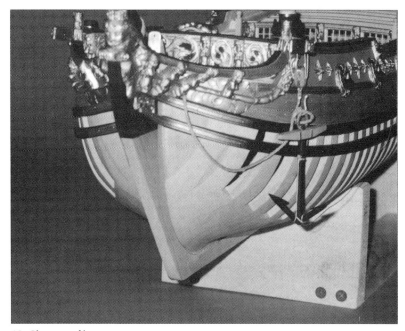

19. Close-up of bow.

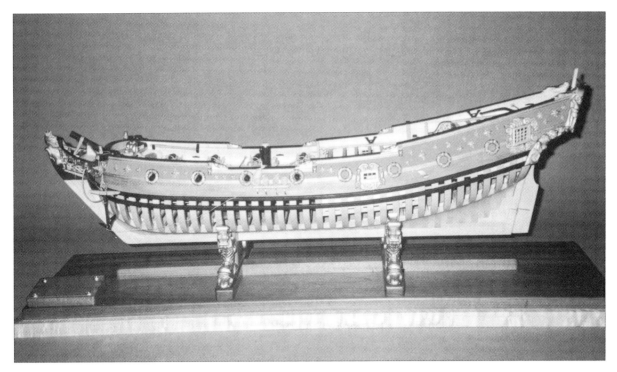

20. The finished hull.

21. Model in its case.

Photographs by the author.

HMS *Constant Reformation* c.1648

by Donald McNarry FRSA

The ship

The *Constant Reformation*, built in 1619, was one of the six Great Ships of James I, all built by William Burrell at Deptford Dockyard.

She had a keel length of 106ft, a beam of 35ft, a depth in hold of 15ft and a tonnage of 750. She was originally built as a 42-gun two-decker.

Together with some of her contemporaries she was later converted to a semi three-decker by decking over the waist thus connecting the forecastle and quarterdeck into one long spar deck.

This enabled her armament to be

Port side view showing hull framing.

increased to between 40 and 60 guns.

The *Constant Reformation* was the flagship of the small Royalist fleet at Hellevoetsluis in Holland in 1648 under the command of Charles I's nephew, Prince Rupert of Bavaria.

She was finally lost at sea in 1651 – quite a long life for a ship of those days.

The data

It can hardly be expected that any useful contemporary plans of a 1619 vessel now exist, however the Society for Nautical Research publication No. 6 includes a set of lines for a somewhat similar ship of c.1620 worked out from contemporary documents by the late Mr W Salisbury. I used these with some adjustment for this *Constant Reformation* model.

There are four drawings of the ship by the elder Van de Velde done in 1648 when the ship was at Hellevoetsluis, two of them at the National Maritime Museum at Greenwich and two at the Boymans Museum, Rotterdam. All show the port side and fortunately two from the bow and two from the stern; two of the drawings seem to be offsets of offsets.

The date 1648 is too early for any known Admiralty Board dockyard models.

The earliest is probably the 1655 two-decker at Greenwich, a model about which there has been much discussion as to whether it is a Royalist ship or originated in Commonwealth times and a Royal Arms added later.

A further early model is in Sweden, traditionally known as Sheldon's *Naseby*, an identification seemingly doubted by some, but probably at least an English-built model.

There are two 'early' models in the Roger's Collection at Annapolis, Nos 50 and 107 in their catalogue. No. 50 is an entirely new work apart from a few of the original carvings and 107 had been interfered with before it went to America and then suffered further depredation.

I have some old photographs of these two models and the change in both is remarkable.

I have written elsewhere that if the Annapolis catalogue of the Roger's Collection is to be taken seriously for purposes of research then prior reading of its reviews in the *Mariner's Mirror* and the American *Neptune* by Dr R C Anderson and Mr W Salisbury is essential.

The Van de Velde drawings though done in 1648, show that the *Constant Reformation* retained many of her early Jacobean characteristics. She had a long, low bow assembly with very upstanding, crowned lion figurehead, entirely unprotected by the head rails as in later years. She had a closed stern but almost Elizabethan single tier quarter galleries, and half open and half closed and glazed. The Van de Veldes show, at the forward end of the gallery, what is almost certainly a toilet, presumably for the afterguard.

There were still traces of the high narrow sterns of the 1500s which added to the vessel's sheer and greatly improved the look of her elevation, the curve of the sheer perhaps being one of the most attractive aspects of most ships, a characteristic sadly lacking in modern architecture.

The model

I built the model as a two-decker and completed the forecastle and quarterdeck bulkheads with their gilded carving and then decked over the waist.

One can have no idea if these

Ornate highly decorated stern.

bulkheads were left in when the *Constant Reformation* was uprated but it seemed likely. As usual it was difficult to relate the flat broadside draught with the perspective three-quarter views of the artist's drawings and in so doing it is important to try and get all deck fittings to look as if they are workable. Ideally the guns should have room to recoil and be withdrawn for loading, room to man the capstan bars, etc.

The three stern lanterns on the ship are not of the same pattern, the centre one being larger and more

Port broadside view of completed model.

Bow and figurehead.

Photographs by the author.

ornate than the other two; indeed it has a very Dutch appearance.

It is interesting to conjecture that the *Constant Reformation* may have lost her own centre lantern and obtained a replacement from the Dutch when at Hellevoetsluis.

It is also interesting to consider how her carving and decoration were treated on the actual ship but on this dockyard model the carving

is all gilded in the usual way for such models. The Van de Velde drawings are of course in black and white but there is some indication that colour was used on the ship especially at the headrails.

Had I done the *Constant Reformation* as a realistic waterline model it would have had a quite different appearance.

I used Dr R C Anderson's *Rigging*

of Ships in the Days of the Spritsail Topmast (1927) exclusively for the masts and rigging.

The case and shelf are of English oak veneer, the plinth has a central panel of oak burr, the rest is figured. The gold rope trim consists of two lengths of left hand lay anchor cable laid up right handed.

The model is to a scale of 26ft = 1in and is 12.5in long. ❏

HMS *Cossack*

A Tribal Class Destroyer

by Mark Slota

Initial inspiration for this miniature came from seeing the two-page centre colour spread at 1:350 scale in *Warship Profile* No. 2 HMS *Cossack* by Lt David Lyon. The scale of the model is also 1:350. Other references used were the 1:192 scale plan of a sister-ship HMS *Matabele* by Norman Ough, *Tribal Class Destroyers* by Peter Hodges, and *British Destroyers* by Edgar March. [*There is also a book* The Tribals *by Martin Brice, published by Ian Allan, London 1971. Ed*]

HMS *Cossack* was built in 1938 by Vickers Armstrong, Wallsend on Tyne. She had an overall length of 377ft and beam of 36.5ft. *Cossack* will always be remembered for the part she played in the rescue of British merchant seamen from the German tanker *Altmark* in Norway in February 1940. She was torpedoed on 22 October 1941, the day after leaving Gibraltar as part of a convoy escort, but sank on 27 October when under tow trying to reach Gibraltar.

I happened to have a discontinued Heller 1:400 scale kit of the French destroyer *Maille Breze*. This was the 1953 one, not the 1930s ship of the same name which sank off Greenock following an on board explosion during the last war. This is the later ship. I found that, though the post-war vessel was some 45ft longer than *Cossack*, this kit hull was only fractionally shorter than that of *Cossack* at 1:350, and that the beam was the same. More to the point, the general characteristics of the two hulls were very similar. I decided to use this Heller hull as a 'donor' hull. The fact that the *Breze's* hull was slightly shorter would allow the bow to be

The finished model, which is about 13in (33cm) long overall.

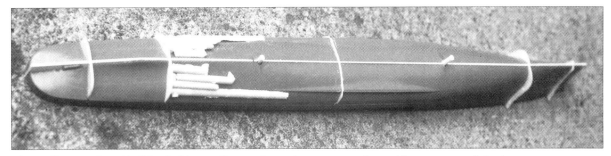

The *Maille Breze* 'donor' hull fitted with centreline member and transverse sections, with some scraps of plastic sprue to act as 'fillers'.

made up to match *Cossack*'s raked stem, and the stern to be modified as necessary.

I began by making a centreline profile and main deck of *Cossack*'s hull, together with a number of transverse sections of the hull from keel to waterline from plasticard. The two halves of the *Maille Breze* hull were firmly glued to the *Cossack* centreline plasticard profile, fol-lowed by the plasticard main deck. Slots (saw cuts) were made in the half hulls from keel to waterline, at the positions for which the section templates had been made.

The cross-section pieces were inserted into the slots, and correctly aligned, and fixed. Plastic padding resin was applied to the hull to fill it out to the shape of the new cross sections and to fair in to the rest of the hull. To save on resin, pieces of scrap plastic sprue were used as fillers. It was sanded smooth, and sheathed with very thin plasticard in which the portholes had been punched.

All the component parts of the deckhouses and superstructure were built up from plasticard. The funnels, torpedo tubes, and other fittings were made up from plastic

Forward part of the model, showing B-gun shield with red, white and blue markings used during the Spanish Civil War, 1938.

'One of the best looking destroyers ever built'. Only 4 of the 16 built survived the war.   *Photographs by the author.*

The model is mounted in turned brass pedestals on a block of pearwood.

tube, rod, and card. The masts were of brass rod, with rigging of blackened copper wire. The gun mountings and ship's boats were cast in resin in silicon rubber moulds, as described in *MS101* ('Making moulded items' by David Collier). To facilitate moulding they are shown fitted with canvas covers. The guard rail stanchions were made from the smallest available entomological pins, 0.005in diameter, and 44swg copper wire, blackened, for the 'rails' (in reality flexible steel wire rope). The only other items from the kit were the propellers. The pendant numbers were 1:72 scale aircraft decals. The model was painted in accordance with the *Warship Profile* details. ❑

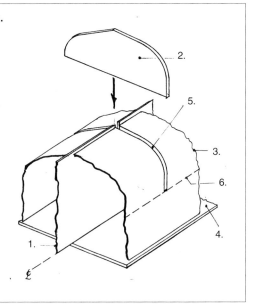

Figure 1. Hull construction.

1. Centreline former cut to *Cossack's* profile.
2. Cross-sections in plasticard of *Cossack's* hull from keel to waterline, taken from body plan.
3. Half hulls glued to *Cossack's* longitudinal centreline profile.
4. Main deck glued in place.
5. Transverse saw cuts from keel to waterline. The plasticard cross-sections will be glued in these slots.
6. Waterline.

HMS *Invincible* (1744–1758)

(Part 2)

by Mark Tindall

Hull planking

One of the traditional rules states that there will not be a butt join on a strake of planking on the same frame which has not been separated by less than four clear strakes – and this is a logical and easily understood piece of reasoning which prevented creating weaknesses in the hull. However, as far as my model was concerned, this also meant that observance of this rule would be difficult since I had fewer frames at my disposal on which to make the joints. However, by careful planning I managed to arrange three divisions of each strake, making each of differing lengths so as to create butts on a frame whilst observing the above rule. A good indication of the whole system is shown in Figure 8a.

So the first length of planking was to be the garboard strake, which also meant the length of planking fitted next to the keel. I decided to complete the planking from the keel up to the first ribband, then to move up the hull to the bulwarks and work towards the centre. I had found that this method produces a strong even hull. Reference to Figure 4 in the last article [*reprinted here for conve-* nience. Ed] shows two bands of planking progressing in this manner.

Incidentally, whilst considering planking it may be as well to mention that there are some well-known modellers who advocate using a double layer of planking on a hull. Their first layer is out of scale in order to form the hull and, in a manner of speaking, to absorb all subsequent fairing and trimming. The second layer would then lie on the first in a very accurate manner, and in such a way using scale width planks, as to cover the longitudinal carvel butts of the first layer. So doing creates a more watertight hull as well as achieving a greater thickness of planking more easily. Whilst I do advocate this method, and am in fact using it on another ship model, I have to say that it is twice the work, although the results are excellent and bending the wood proved to be much easier. As mentioned previously, I did not use this method on *Invincible* when making the ribbands above, preferring to bend the wood wet at the correct thickness around a hot forming tool as described.

This is all very subjective and it is

up to the modeller to decide which is the better method. I have used both successfully although in all cases the hull was subsequently sealed inside with a coat of glass fibre resin, which effectively watertights most wooden hulls.

The way of marking each length of prepared planking will be similar, although the shapes will vary considerably. The plank widths having been marked on each former as described previously it only remains to transfer these marks on to the appropriate length of planking and cut them to shape. This shape is the edge next to the keel or an upper plank. Following this the plank is bent and fitted in position. To do this, a length of planking is offered up to the hull and on to this is marked the position of each former. The appropriate widths are then marked off for that particular plank, using proportional dividers or a simple strip of paper, and transferred on to the plank at the particular frame position. A pencil line drawn through the marks will give the shape of the plank at each former. This has then to be shaped to the line. Here methods vary. I prefer to clamp the plank between two strips of wood kept for the purpose, clamp

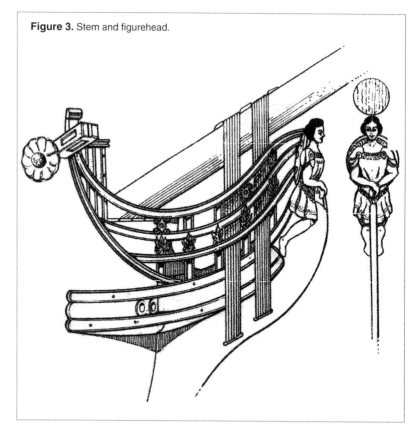

Figure 3. Stem and figurehead.

the whole assembly in the vice, and plane the edge to the pencil line. This can be done with an ordinary block plane.

Where an extreme curve is required I use either a compass plane or, if the wood is not too wide and I wish to preserve the grain around the curvature, I will bend it to the shape using the previously mentioned bending iron, and bend the wood across its width. This is a skilled operation, but it is a skill well worth developing, as the advantages of preserving the grain direction around a curve are many. This should be clear from Figures 8a, 8b and 8c.

Having the first plank cut out and finished to its correct widths at each former, I looked at it to see exactly where it curved, and thus decide if an inward bend would be necessary.

I assessed, simply by looking, exactly where this particular strake curved in order to decide whether an inward bend would be required. I have found that the planking assumes the rough shapes shown in Figure 10a. The first drawing shows a normal plank about the bilge area

Figure 4. Planking in progress on inverted hull.

Figure 8a. Arrangement of plank butts.

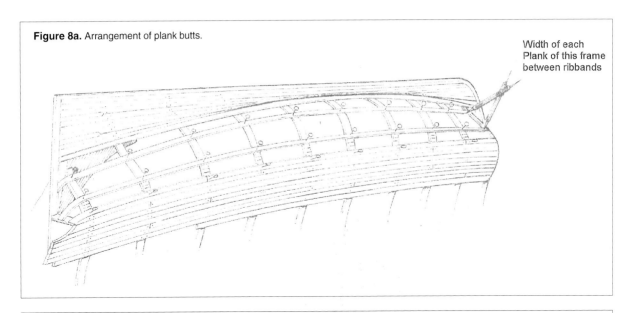

Width of each
Plank of this frame
between ribbands

Figures 8b & 8c.
Plank preparation.

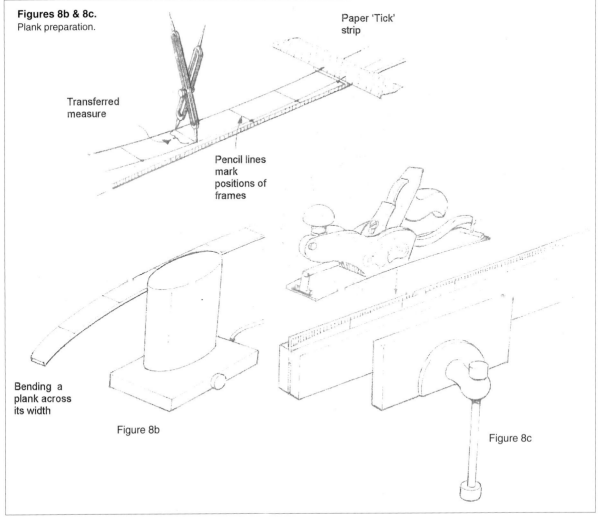

Paper 'Tick'
strip

Transferred
measure

Pencil lines
mark
positions of
frames

Bending a
plank across
its width

Figure 8b

Figure 8c

of the ship. Additionally, at each end, an inwards curve in varying degrees was required to fit the end curves of the hull. This was done on the bending iron tool after wetting the wood. Thus from time to time a strake of planking could contain a complex curve in two directions, and even have a twist imparted at either end of the hull. Having offered up the completed shape to the keel, and decided that it fitted correctly and was in contact with all the markings on the formers, I secured it in place with planking pins. In this case the garboard strake usually goes on in one length and not three as is normal. These pins (illustrated) are made from paper clips. The diameter of one of these clips is 1.2mm which corresponds with a common size of mini drill, and such a drill was fitted into a small hand held pin chuck. Later, these pinholes would be filled with a treenail made from bamboo. I make all my treenails with the aid of a drawplate.

I carried on with the planking, alternating from one side of the hull to the other to ensure a balanced structure without twists. I worked as shown from the garboard band and then from the bulwarks towards the centre until the last plank was to be put in. The only difference in procedure here was that both edges of the plank had to be marked and worked in order to fit this last one into position. It was an advantage to put a slight bevel on each edge of the plank to ensure a good fit. Incidentally, when one surface is to fit perfectly to another along their respective lengths, this is called 'faying'. The surface in contact is known as the 'faying surface' (see Figure 10).

As each three strakes of planking were fitted on each side of the vessel the hull shape began to take on an even more pleasing appearance and greatly encouraged further efforts. At this point, after two strakes per side had been pinned, I removed the first strake of three, placed them on the

Figure 9a. The port side of the hull showing wales and gun ports.

Figure 9b. Port quarter view of the model set on its temporary stand.

bench in sequence, then did the same with the other two lengths of one side of the hull. I applied Cascamite and pinned each piece of planking in place, wiping any surplus glue from the joints, then did the same for the other side of the hull. While these were drying I continued marking, shaping, fitting, and pinning the remaining planks until the last plank was fitted as described above.

I could now remove the hull from the building board and frames. This was done by unscrewing all former retaining screws from the underside of the structure and then unscrewing the small pieces which held the two halves of the formers in position. I could now view the hull properly the right way up and clear of its building board. I made a very simple working stand for the model by transferring

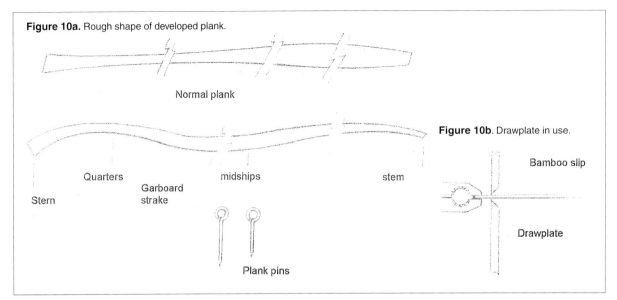

Figure 10a. Rough shape of developed plank.

Normal plank

Stern
Quarters
Garboard strake
midships
stem

Plank pins

Figure 10b. Drawplate in use.

Bamboo slip

Drawplate

the shape of two suitable hull cross sections on to cardboard, and cutting these to form templates to put the shape on to two pieces of plywood. When cut out these were joined to each other by two long rails screwed in place. This can be seen in the photograph marked Figure 9. The inner surfaces of the stand on which the hull would rest were lined with cork stuck on with Evostik. The cork was part of a widely available type of floor tile, an invaluable item to have around for it has many uses, not the least of which is lining sanding tools before gluing on abrasive papers.

Part of the process of taking off the formers is to remove the screws holding the frames to them at the base of the structure and, with a

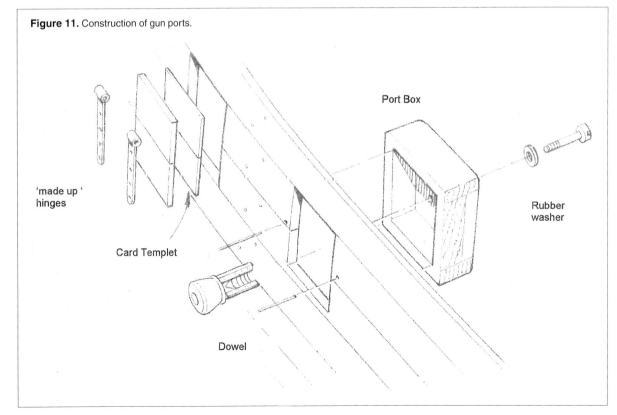

Figure 11. Construction of gun ports.

Port Box

'made up' hinges

Card Templet

Rubber washer

Dowel

short flexible saw, cut them down to the level of the bulwarks.

The hull planking being completed and faired to my satisfaction using a spoke shave and sanding tools, I ran additional strakes on to the hull at the position of the wales to bring them up to the required thickness. These positions were plotted from the body plan and taken off on to pieces of cardboard, after which they were cut out so that I could offer them up to the hull and transfer the plots on to the hull. I joined these with a pencil line, using a long thin flexible batten as a guide, and which I had previously bent to the correct curvature. It was easy to work to this line when fitting and pinning the wales in position.

Inspection of the hull when this work was finished revealed that some minor adjustments in fairing were needed and these were made. The hull now looked very good. At this point I decided to paint the wales black.

The gun ports were the next consideration. I prepared long battens, much the same as the one used to mark the wale position, but to the line following the gun ports on the profile drawing (which was the full size of the model). On these I marked every gun port for each deck on a separate batten. For this operation, the batten was temporarily fixed to the hull in the correct position, using masking tape, whilst the ports were being marked on both sides of the hull. The full shape of each port was subsequently drawn in.

The next job was to cut out the gun port openings, even though I had decided that those on the gun deck would be closed. My reason was that a correctly made and fitted gun port lid glued in the closed position would look more realistic than one which had been marked or scored in. Of course this would necessitate a thorough watertighting of the hull. This cutting operation had to be done with care, as any inaccuracy would result in an ugly out of alignment gun port. The outline of each port was cut in with a scalpel and straightedge. Next a skewed (angled) chisel was used to cut up to this line and, with the waste removed, thus formed a very accurately V-shaped groove, which effectively delineated each port. By continuing cutting and grooving the aperture was gradually cut through and the middle section came away, leaving a very clean edged port. This can be seen in the photographs. The hull had been given a finishing coat at this stage, and the rudder cut out and fitted with brass pintles which were finished in black. All metalwork on a man-of-war was usually

Hull planking in progress.

black, which can be represented either by painting the metal with enamel paint, or chemically blackening it, touching up any wear with paint. I have used both methods successfully.

The finish is very important for a sailing model, and I had no intention of covering up the beautiful planking with paint. As this was not done at the period in question in any case for the space between the wales, the only finish possible had to be high quality yacht varnish. I should mention that there seems to be a popular misconception that matt yacht varnish works in the same way as the glossy variety. This simply is not true, the watertighting qualities are only present in the gloss finish varnish (this information is available from the technical department of specialist suppliers).

As making the gun port lids and their fittings would be a long job, I decided to divide my time between these, constructing the head rails, and work on the stern. I have to say that this method of working can be very beneficial when a long repetitive job has to be undertaken.

The diagram, Figure 12, shows how I made the gun port lids, and the furniture for them, and the box which had to be secured behind each open port to help ensure a watertight hull. It will be seen that this small box was also the means whereby I could secure the cannon spiggots and at the same time remain watertight. Later, the interior of the hull would be coated with a layer of glass fibre resin just to make sure. Originally I had not made these cannons as spigots, having decided to my cost to mount them correctly on a deck and have them showing in all their glory. This proved to be a bad mistake, as the ship heeled over quite a lot because I wanted it to carry full sail. I realised that spigots would give just the same effect as the remainder of the cannon could not be seen in any case. They have proved to be most successful.

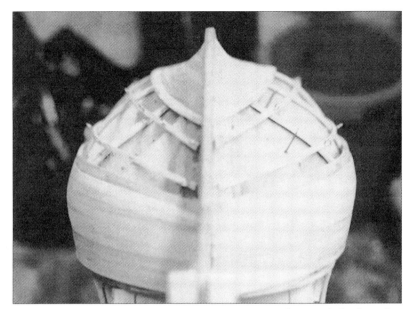

Showing hull construction.

Photographs by the author.

I had decided to have the upper deck cannons showing, and to close the gun deck ports as previously stated. This meant that I would need 28 boxes and 28 gun port lids on hinges. It also meant that I would need another 28 gun port lids with hinges for the closed ports, but these would not need boxes as the lids would be in the closed position. I would also need 28 spigot cannons in brass, and 16 cannons on the forecastle and quarterdeck. These latter would have to be fully detailed, with carriages.

Each port had to have an accurately fitting lid. I made a card template for each one, including the closed ports. Having fitted them into their appropriate ports, I marked out on each one the exact positions of the adjoining planks, which must follow the lines or sheer of the planking. I selected matching planking offcuts of similar colouring and glued these together so as to cover the maximum depth of the appropriate deck's gun ports. By offering up each template in turn, I could mark the exact shape of that port on it and cut it out. Very little trimming was necessary and this procedure was carried out for all remaining ports –

in between other jobs. A small but vital point about gun ports is that each port and anything made for it must be given and marked with an identifying number. Failure to do this can cause much inconvenience.

I felt that it would be better for the sake of authenticity if the lower (closed) gun ports were fitted with all the necessary furniture. Strangely, even from a distance, these ports look as though they are open, perhaps because the furniture on them is black. The method I used to produce the hinges and pintles is shown in Figure 12. All joints were silver soldered throughout .

The sides of the hull still had a daunting amount of work to be done. This included the channels with all their associated parts, such as links, the gun port rigols, and the remaining mouldings, all of which I could return to later.

I turned now to producing patterns for, and making a start on the cheeks at the head (stem), following which I would do the same with the head rails. After making my first attempt at the cheeks, I had to discard the entire effort as it turned out to be nothing like I had intended. A glance at Figure 13 (an appropriate number) reveals a complex curve in two directions. The same thing happens with the hull planking, but this is much thinner material. I had read of other modellers carving these shapes out of a solid piece of timber, but I could not bring myself to waste this amount of material (to me this is always a cardinal sin!). After some experimenting the situation resolved itself into a bending exercise, as will be clear from studying Figure 14. The material for the cheeks was sycamore, a marvellous, hard and very bendable wood grown in England.

The components of the first two rails below the head are called the upper and lower cheeks. The upper one blends as it rises into another rail called the hair bracket. On *Invincible* these surround the hawse hole area which houses the holes for the anchor cable. This is contrary to English practice where the hawse holes are usually above these rails. Reference to Figure 3 in the first article [*but repeated here for convenience. Ed*] shows these components clearly – in fact the figurehead has her feet resting on them.

The first requirement was to make and fit a template of the cheeks which ensured their perfect contact with the hull. This template was used to mark out the shape of the upper cheek on to a piece of sycamore, which had been jointed in two pieces in order to have the grains running as nearly as possible in the direction of the whole shape, as can be seen in Figure 13a. This joint was glued flat on to a piece of glass or melamine covered wood, which had been rubbed with a candle to prevent gluing the work to the surface. Following this, the joint was dowelled using one length of dowel, Figure 10b, and lightly tapped in place with a small pin hammer, cut off, and trimmed flush with a scalpel.

This cheek, still flat, had to be bent upwards in a predetermined curve to fit on to the stem. Figure 13a shows that it has to fit exactly to the rising curve of the stem. I just bent the card template to fit this curve and then soaked the assembly and gradually bent the cheek to conform to the shape. This is shown in Figure 13b, but it is fairly difficult to show the upward tilt of the shape – it is necessary to imagine an even steeper curve. (This could have been drawn but was not in order to keep the diagram simple and the construction easily understood.)

Now a moulding has to go on to the edge of this assembly. This procedure is identical for all of the head rails. I did this using a very handy home-made tool. Figure 14 shows a piece of sycamore in a vice. The wood is the correct thickness for the width of the cheek. A hand tool is made, comprising two pieces of rectangular timber of suitable length for the hand, for example, about the size of a spokeshave. The inner faces must be absolutely flat. Four holes are drilled around the periphery of a slot which is fashioned as shown and these are counterbored to suit a 4BA cheesehead screw or a metric equivalent. The reverse of the bores are also counterbored to suite the nuts for the screws. A tool blade is made from a piece of hacksaw blade or from an old handsaw to the shape shown. Sharpened in the manner illustrated, this blade is pinched squarely into the tool so as to leave an edge against which the tool locates on to the sycamore plank. With the bevelled edge of the blade nearest to the craftsman the tool is worked to and fro from the furthest end of the plank towards the front until a nice

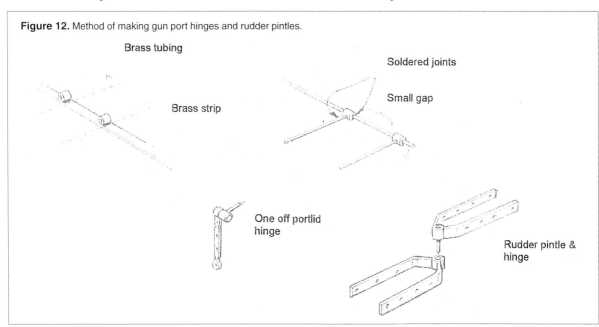

Figure 12. Method of making gun port hinges and rudder pintles.

Brass tubing

Brass strip

Soldered joints

Small gap

One off portlid hinge

Rudder pintle & hinge

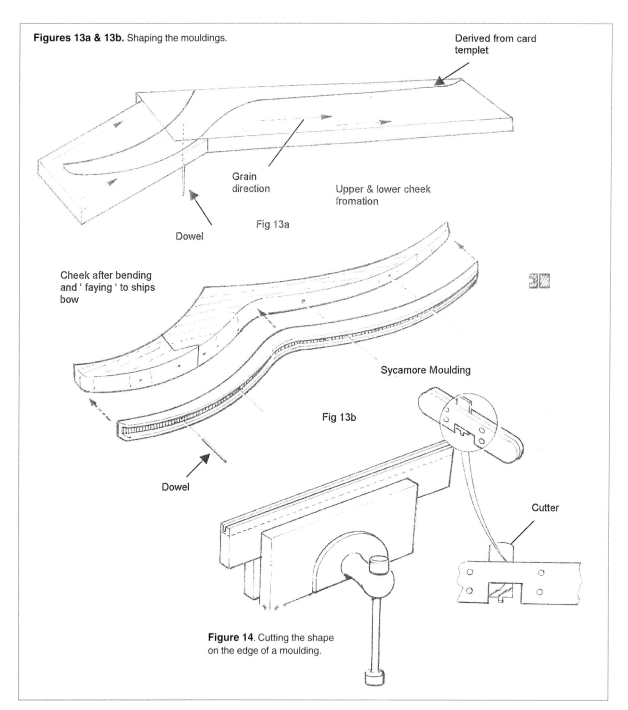

Figures 13a & 13b. Shaping the mouldings.

Derived from card templet

Grain direction

Upper & lower cheek fromation

Dowel

Fig 13a

Cheek after bending and ' faying ' to ships bow

Sycamore Moulding

Fig 13b

Dowel

Cutter

Figure 14. Cutting the shape on the edge of a moulding.

moulded groove is achieved. The plank is then removed from the vice and a marking gauge used to mark the depth of the moulding, after which it is cut from the plank. This is cleaned up with garnet paper to achieve a smooth finish and to round the edges of the forward face of the

moulding. After soaking, the moulding is carefully bent on the bending iron or soldering iron until in perfect contact with the edge of the cheek assembly, as described and shown in Figure 13b. It is then glued, pinned and dowelled in the usual manner. The lower cheek was made in the

same way and then both assemblies were in turn pinned, glued and dowelled to the stem at the correct pitch, see Figure 3.

(The next article will deal with making the head rails and the stern galleries).

to be continued. ❏

The Grimsay Double-ender

Some thoughts on its design

by Donald A MacQuarrie

Following my article in *MS119* on a model of this boat, some readers may have wondered: 'Where did the shape of the Grimsay boat come from?' The design of the east coast herring fleet (Scaffies, Fifies and Zulus) probably owed their design more to the influences from the Continent rather than Scandinavia. Similarly the Loch Fyne Skiff, which also fished for herring, has many similarities with the Zulu which was so successful in fishing the North Sea and the west coast.

It is easy to see the influence of the Vikings on the Shetland boats and in the design of the Sgoth Niseach. So what were the roots of the Grimsay boat which had its beginnings in the early 1800s and served its community to the end of the twentieth century and beyond? This is truly a remarkable and unique achievement among boat builders, not only in the Western Isles but also throughout all our coasts.

What designs or influences were about at that time? The Stewarts first came to North Uist in 1803 from Appin in Argyll to work as house

Figure 1. Where did the shape of the Grimsay boat come from?

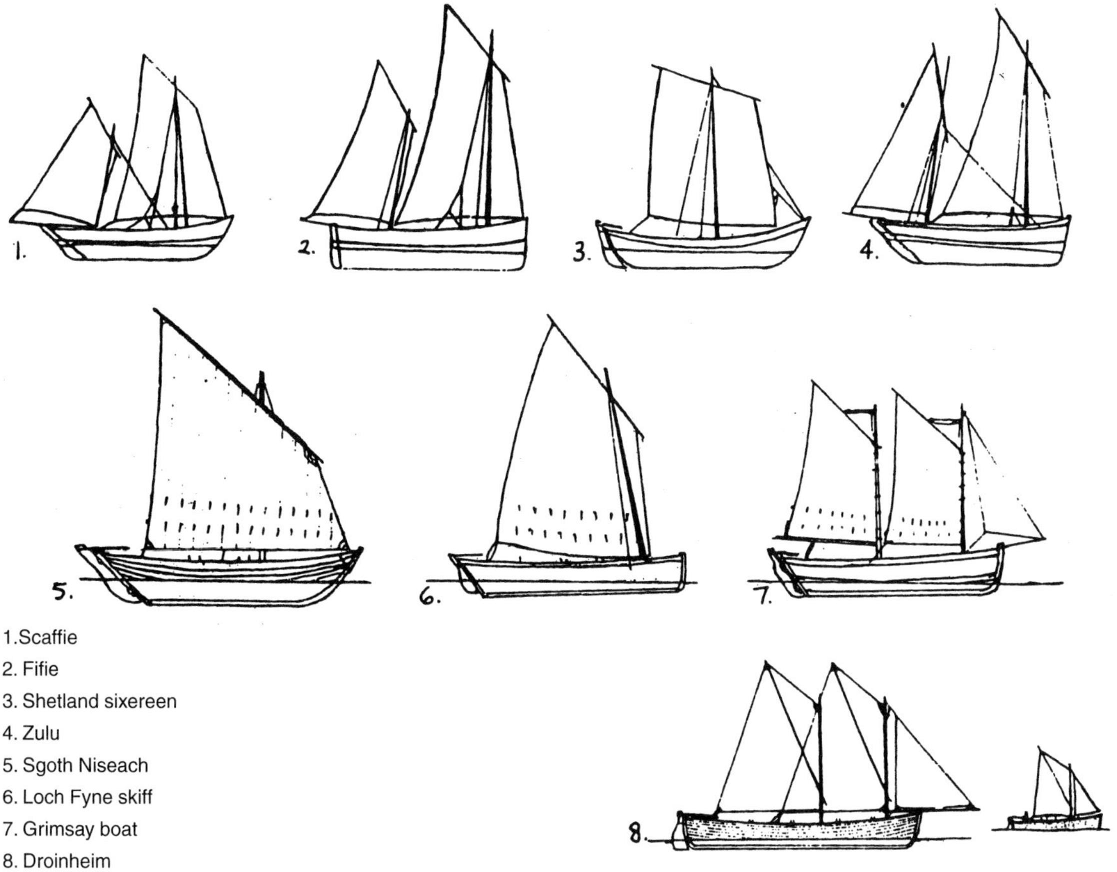

1. Scaffie
2. Fifie
3. Shetland sixereen
4. Zulu
5. Sgoth Niseach
6. Loch Fyne skiff
7. Grimsay boat
8. Droinheim

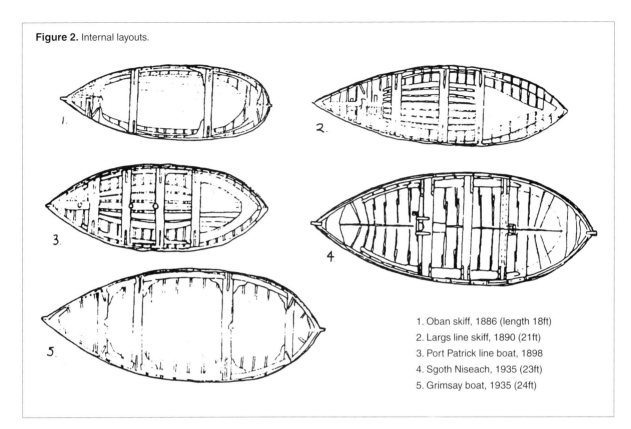

Figure 2. Internal layouts.

1. Oban skiff, 1886 (length 18ft)
2. Largs line skiff, 1890 (21ft)
3. Port Patrick line boat, 1898
4. Sgoth Niseach, 1935 (23ft)
5. Grimsay boat, 1935 (24ft)

builders in Lochmaddy, but soon started to build boats in Grimsay.

Materials were hard to come by in Uist since there were no trees and any small boats such as they were, were imported from the mainland or came on the decks of sailing ships, or were sold by the herring fleets at the end of the season. There is no evidence of boat kits, such as the ones that were imported to Shetland and Ireland from Norway, coming to Uist, but it is quite possible that assembled boats from these kits reached the Western Isles. The two Amsted Droinheim, as used on the north coast of Ireland and on Islay, may have influenced the double-mast on the boats in Uist.

Birlinns and the Lord of the Isles

It is important to mention that there was a time when there was a very strong local seagoing tradition on the western seaboard of Scotland. This was the era of the Lord of the Isles, when the clan chiefs ruled the

waters and the islands using the Highland galley, the Birlinn. This was a period in the history of the west coast, which is slowly being revealed as a time of extraordinary activity, resulting in a rich culture with powerful political and religious influences.

The Birlinn had a long and distinguished pedigree, since it was a direct descendent of the Viking longboat. To date no Birlinn or even part of one has ever been found, but we can vouch for its seaworthiness through the poems and songs of the bards, and we are well acquainted with its streamlined form and its rigging through stone carvings on gravestones. No doubt the shape of the Birlinn in their own day varied according to the criteria of locality, use (cargo or war galley), and sea conditions.

What becomes clear is that a community dependent on the sea will be proud to call a boat type their own. Perhaps its shape and form enters

into the psyche as much as does the associated stories and folklore about fishing and sailing.

Many a fishing community would not take kindly to a boat of a different design. Such a design would be recognised as a 'foreigner' in their midst.

The Grimsay double-ender of the early 1900s no doubt developed from many influences, not least the small boats that accompanied and served the herring industry. Since the hull form and profile do not portray any immediate Scandinavian influences (apart from clinker build), it might be assumed that the shape which became so pleasing to local eyes had its roots in the small work boats of Ayrshire, the north coast of Ireland, the Isle of Man and Argyll.

The east coast of Scotland is proud of its Fifies, Scaffies and Zulus. Shetland is proud of her Sixereens. Orkney and Fair Isle are proud of their Yoles. Lewis is proud of her Sgoth Niseach. Argyll is proud

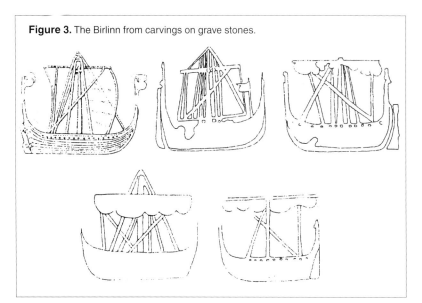

Figure 3. The Birlinn from carvings on grave stones.

of her Loch Fyne Skiffs. North Uist is proud of her Eathar Griomasaigh (Grimsay boat).

In the 1930s a Devon man, Philip Oke, was commissioned to take the lines from traditional workboats around the coast of the United Kingdom. In Scotland he took the lines from traditional boats from Solway to Oban. What a pity he did not make it out to the Uists. However, the work he did was invaluable, and it could be inferred that the shape of these boats and their predecessors from Ayrshire, Largs, Ardrishaig, and Oban were related to the Grimsay boat.

A common feature is the rounded full stern that depended on the local working conditions and the typical size of a following sea.

The Grimsay boat was originally designed for lobster fishing and transportation around the coasts of Uist and in particular the Monach Isles (6 miles west of Uist). The weather conditions and the work demanded a seaworthy, stable boat that was strong in construction and easy to handle.

The Grimsay boat contains these valuable features:

(i) a keel construction where the first few planks effectively extend the depth of the keel. When ballasted, usually with stones, this provided good stability.

(ii) the reinforcement of the knees between each of the thwarts by a length of shelf (though not common on every boat). In effect this created a strong reinforcing ring near the inside gunnel of the boat. This feature is rare on Southern skiffs and is not to be found in the boats of the Northern Isles.

(iii) a fine stem entry with graceful underwater lines and a fulsome sweeping stern.

One reason why the Grimsay boat design has been so enduring and remained a practical workboat is the fact that an engine could be installed without great difficulty and without detriment to the boat's sailing abilities. This was not so for the east coast Zulus or the Sgoth Niseach because of their acutely raked sterns.

Conclusion

It is probably an over simplification to suggest that the Grimsay boat evolved from a type of skiff common to the fishing communities of the west coast of Scotland while the shape of the Sgoth Niseach (see

MS99) from Lewis clearly derives from Scandinavian influences. However, it may well be that for small workboats at least, the long island is the locus where north meets south. That is, where the fishing communities in the southern half of the Western Isles in their thinking at least, were more comfortable with a west coast design, whereas the northern part were much more at home with a boat of Scandinavian design.

Could it be that this is where Celtic meets Norse in small boat design?

'thatched homes have been replaced by modern houses;

horse and cart has been replaced by tractor and 4 x 4;

fibre glass, plastic and steel have replaced wood;

yet larch and oak will always be there to make fine boats'

Wooden boats will always draw a wondering eye. They cause little pollution in the making and good forestry and nature will replace the oak and larch for the next generation to enjoy.

The story of Grimsay's boats is a story of skill and pride, of humility and humanity, and great achievement often in the face of difficulties and harsh weather conditions.

I have spoken about a particular small wooden traditional working boat at a particular time and in a particular place. However, it is essentially a story about a people and their community, about husbands and wives striving, and children painting their little boats and sailing them on the tide – and sometimes loosing them.

If, even in some small way, a traditional boat like the Grimsay boat can help to remind us of these basic human values then they deserve to be preserved and even copied for generations yet to come. ❏

Steam Tug Coringa

(Part 3)

by R Halleron

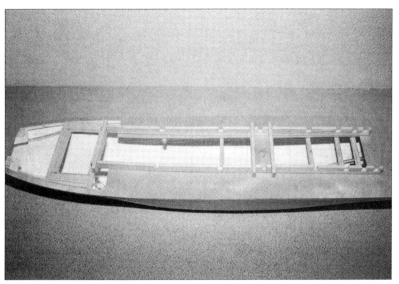

14. Access framework.

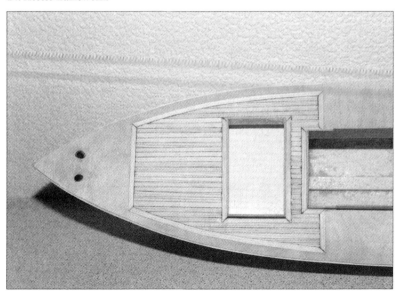

Fitting the access framework and coaming

To provide extra strength and support to any access openings a wooden framework is fitted beneath the deck to the exact dimensions of the final access opening. The underside of the deck is curved not only across but also along the boat. In order to obtain the correct curvature use a piece of card, initially with a straight edge, placed where the framework will fit. With a pencil attached to a wooden block run a line along the card parallel to the deck in a manner similar to a depth or marking gauge. After cutting the card check against the deck for correct curvature. This card template can now be used to produce the wooden framework the depth of which should be at least twice the thickness of a deck beam to allow sufficient wood for keying into the deck beams as shown in Photograph 14. Note that the pieces which run across the hull are jointed into those which run along the hull for added strength. A support structure has also been built around the forward access to give something to which the planks can be glued, see Photograph 14.

Once the framework has been glued in place below the deck any waste must be removed from the inside of the opening so that it becomes flush with the framework. A coaming must now be glued to the support framework and deck over which the superstructure will fit. To obtain the correct curvature for the coaming, use the same card template as was used for the support framework. The height of the coaming will depend upon the superstructure, but try to make it as high as possible to give the maximum water protection. When using Resin W, or a similar, weatherproof glue, it helps to run a fillet of glue all round the coaming at deck level for added water protection, see Figure 15.

15. Planked deck at the bow.

The planked deck area can now be fitted, using similar planks to those used on the hull. Start by fitting an edging strip, or margin plank, to the outer area, and round the access opening. The inner part can now be filled, a plank at a time, using Resin W glue. To emphasise the joint (i.e., simulate the caulking) the edges of each plank were coloured with a black permanent ink felt tip marker pen. Once all planks were fitted and the glue dry, they were sanded to a smooth finish level with the rest of the deck, but making due allowance for the camber. The finished result is shown in Photograph 15. Figure 15 shows a cross section in way of an access opening.

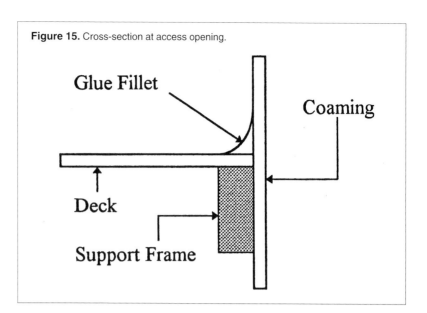

Figure 15. Cross-section at access opening.

Fitting the bulwarks

Step 1. The bulwarks are made from 1.5mm (¹⁄₁₆in) ply wood. From the edge of the hull mark a groove along the deck where the bulwark will stand. The gap between hull edge and line should be a pencil line over the thickness of the wood used for the bulwark. For best results use a marking gauge with a sharp point. Remove this thin strip of deck to form a rebate into which the bulwark will fit. See Figure 16.

Step 2: Make a card rectangle much wider than the height of the bulwark, and a few centimetres longer. Using masking tape attach the card to the side of the hull where the bulwark will be fitted. Because of the sheer and shape of the hull, the rectangular card will not fit into the rebate; this is intentional. The card should be placed on the outside of the hull, and attached so that its lower edge is below deck level at the bow and stern. Using a pencil draw a line along the inside of the card at deck level. Cut along the line and check that the template thus formed fits accurately into the rebate for the bulwark cut in the hull. Draw a second pencil line on the card parallel with the first at a distance away equal to the height of the bulwark

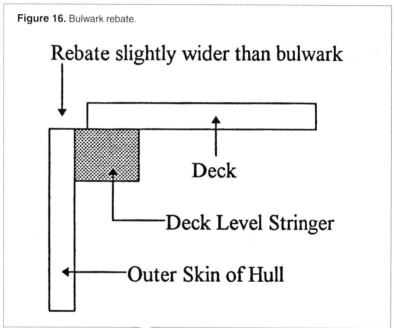

Figure 16. Bulwark rebate.

above the deck plus the depth of the rebate. Use this template to cut the bulwarks from the 1.5mm ply, and fit in place.

Step 3. The stern section of the bulwark is made in one piece and secured to the two side pieces using an lap joint. It should be made as described in step two but about 30mm (1.25in) longer than the curved section of the stern in order to provide the required overlap at each end with the side bulwarks. It may be necessary to steam the wood using boiling water and an old tea towel. Note: the stern bulwark slopes inwards and so the piece of wood used to make it must be wider at the centre than at the ends to maintain a level top once in place. This is not difficult if done at the card template stage. A block of wood with a pencil secured at the

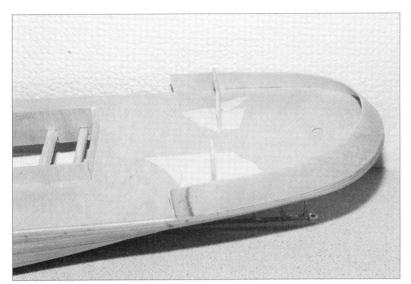

16. Attaching bulwarks, stern view.

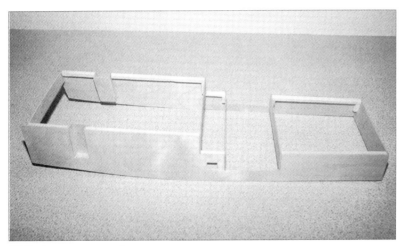

17. Basic superstructure frame.

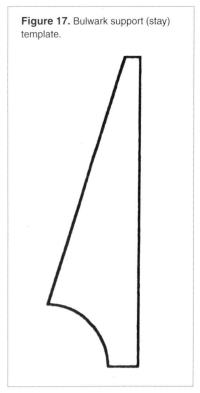

Figure 17. Bulwark support (stay) template.

correct height can be used to mark the top of the bulwark on the card while it is taped to the outside of the hull and held in the correct configuration.

Step 4. Before gluing the bulwark in place several supports must be cut from thick card. These are needed to give the correct rake to the bulwark. The angle of rake can be taken from the cross section of the vessel shown on the plans.

The supports must be firmly attached to the deck in the correct position to hold the bulwark. Each end of the stern bulwark must be

chamfered to form the overlap joint with the side pieces. Using Resin W weather proof glue secure the centre section only of the stern bulwarks. Once the centre section is dry secure each end. Gluing in two stages is much easier when trying to bend the wood at the same time. The ends of this stern bulwark must be fitted inside the ends of the side bulwarks.

Before gluing the side sections the overlapping joints must be prepared. Dry fit the unglued sections and mark where they overlap the stern piece. Chamfer the inner edge of the loose section so that when they overlap a flush joint is produced. Secure

the side bulwark again using card supports to obtain the correct rake. Photograph 16 shows the stern bulwark.

Step 5. A few items are required to complete the bulwark. The first of these are upright supports, better known as bulwark stays. A suggested shape is given in Figure 17.

The angle at the point is the same as the rake of the bulwark and the arched cut-out at the base can be made quite easily. Before gluing the supports in place the freeing ports must be marked and cut out. As this is a working model it might be wise to make these slightly over scale size to facilitate clearing any water from the deck. Ensure that the supports are evenly spaced, and kept clear of the freeing ports, and are vertical rather than at 90 degrees to the deck.

Step 6. The top of the bulwark has to be fitted with a capping rail (usually this is an angle bar or a bulb angle, with the longer flange horizontal and the shorter one placed on the outboard side of the bulwark plate and secured to it). This capping rail can be made from lengths of plywood.

Begin by making a card template. Secure the card to the top of the bulwark and mark its outline on the card. Cut along the pencil line to give a curve which matches the bulwark. Using this template cut out lengths of capping rail just a fraction over the scale width of ⅛in (3mm) from 1.5mm (¹⁄₁₆in) plywood. The bow section is better made in the form of a U-shaped piece of plywood rather than trying to snape the ends of the rail to form a join at the stem head. The length of rail has to be glued to the top of the bulwark with the outer edge flush with the outside of the bulwark.

Leave about 20mm (¾in) either side of any joint loose, overlapping the rail at these points. To make the joint where two pieces of rail overlap, use a sharp knife to cut through both pieces of wood together. Once all pieces are glued and jointed the inside and outside edge should be sanded smooth.

Step 7. Other items which can be added at this stage are Samson posts from brass rod, mooring rings from rings or ovals of plywood with one layer removed and sanded flat on top with chamfered sides.

Hull fender

There is a heavy timber fender all round the hull at deck level. The fender is made from three strips having the same dimensions as hull planks, but long enough to pass all around the hull in one piece.

The fender is fitted with the top edge level with the deck, see Figure 18.

The three pieces have to be glued in place one at a time, starting at the bow in each case. Begin by gluing part way down one side. When this has dried glue around the stern, continuing to the bow after the glue has set.

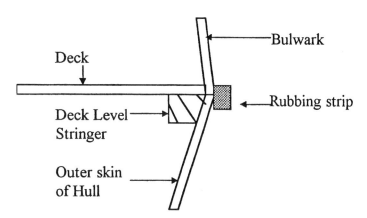

Figure 18. Fitting fender to hull.

Superstructure

As mentioned earlier, the superstructure is made as two removable sections. The basic shapes must be drawn on card, taking the sizes from the plan. Each section should be built first in card, so that any minor adjustments can be made and mistakes corrected before moving to cutting material.

Build up the superstructure so that it is a loose fit over the coaming fixed to the deck. The loose fit can always be made tighter once all the painting, etc. has been done. A tight fit at this early stage will prevent the superstructure fitting after paint has been applied. When satisfied with the card templates their outlines must be transferred to the build material, 1.5mm (¹⁄₁₆ in) plywood.

Before gluing the pieces together it is advantageous to increase the surface area of the glue contact points by fitting pieces of wood or plastic card as appropriate. Photograph 17 illustrates this point. (Note: this is not *Coringa* but the principle is the same).

The rounded corners on the

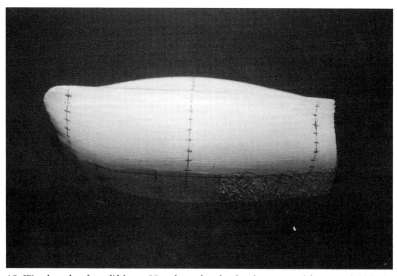

18. Wooden plug for a lifeboat. Note how the plug has been carved from a solid block of wood, and a series of marks placed at bow, centre and stern to help with plank alignment.

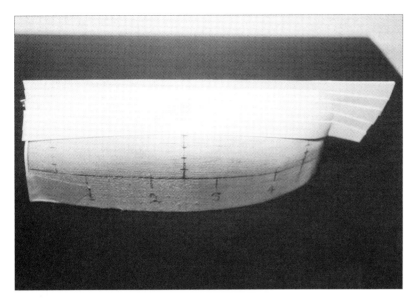

19. First few planks of a clinker lifeboat. The stern has been cut out and secured with masking tape. The first five planks on each side have been glued in place. Note how the planks have been crimped at the bow and the excess material there glued together. The numbers which can be seen below the line indicating the top of the boat were used to shape the plug and mark the points for which card templates were made. When all planks have been fitted, the shell of the boat can be removed from the plug. The result can be seen in Photograph 20.

20. Boat shell after removal from plug. The stern must be cut to size and the top given a slightly convex curve. Any excess plastic must be removed from the bow, following the line formed by crimping the plastic together, but leaving a gap of about 1mm to prevent the bow coming unglued. The keel should be reinforced by adding a narrow strip of 1mm thick plastic card inside and outside of the hull. The top plank, i.e. the gunwale, has to have a strip of wood half the width of this plank fitted all round on the inside, its top being level with the top edge of the plank. The outside of this plank has to be fitted with a double thickness of 1mm plastic card 2mm wide; the grab ropes will be secured to this later. The interior should be fitted with timbers (frames), floorboards, thwarts, etc., as shown in Photographs 21 and 22.

bridge house can be made by fitting a solid block at the corner and trimming to shape once all the pieces are in place. Remember that the deck has both sheer and camber, so the bottom of the deckhouses must be shaped to suit these curves. The card template made when building the coaming support may come in handy here.

There are a few additional points to mention before moving on to deck fittings.

1. The bridge deck is planked like the main deck. The planks should be fitted on the ply deck after the bridge house sides and ends have been erected. As before, one edge of each plank has been blackened using a waterproof marker pen.

2. All port holes, doors and hatches have been cut out and, with the exception of port holes, lined with a very thin plywood called *miralite*, which is about 0.5mm (½in) thick.

3. The bulwark on the bridge is made in exactly the same way as that on the hull, but covered on both sides with thin strips of veneer to simulate vertical planks.

4. To make painting easier, leave off the bridge house roof.

Each funnel was made from a single piece of *miralite* plywood chamfered on each end to form an overlapping joint, rolled round a former (which came from the centre of a roll of fax paper), and glue with Resin W. To prevent the funnels sticking to the former the latter should be wrapped in greaseproof paper. Once dry remove the former and sand the base

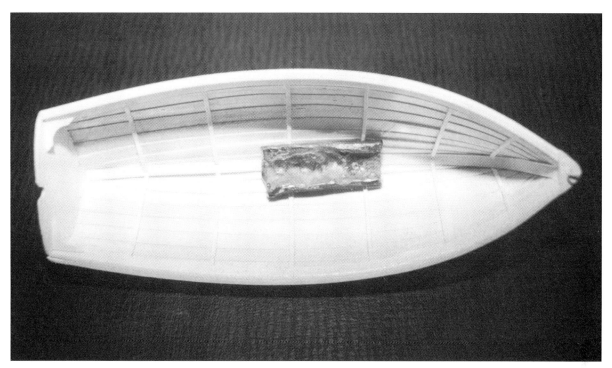

21. Interior, showing timbers (frames).

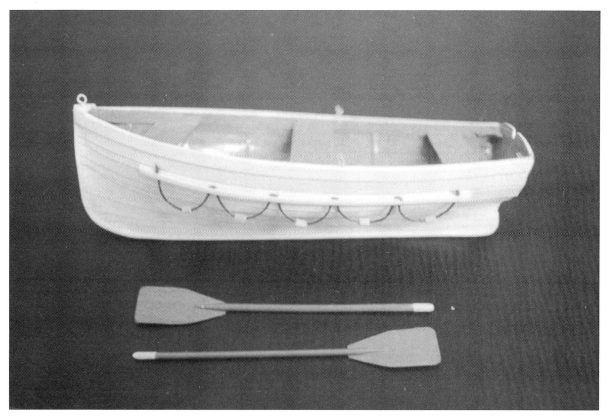

22. Clinker lifeboat completed.

Photographs by the author.

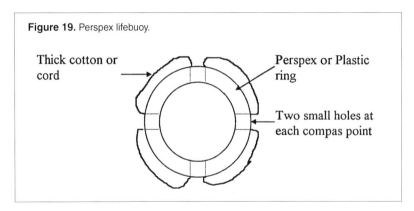

Figure 19. Perspex lifebuoy.

Thick cotton or cord

Perspex or Plastic ring

Two small holes at each compas point

to the correct rake. The bands at the top were made from brass rod bent and silver soldered together. The base of each funnel was thickened on the outside with a piece of 1.5mm (1⁄16in) plywood wrapped round and sanded to shape.

Deck fittings

Deck fittings can be made from a variety of materials. When deciding on which items to make and the material(s) to be used, there are a few points to consider.

1. Will the item be handled, require to be functional and so need to be strong?
2. Is the item tall or large, and need to be light to keep down top weight and not have an effect on stability?
3. How will the item be made, does it require bolts or gearwheels, thus indicating brass or other metal in its construction, or does it have a complicated shape more easily carved from wood?

Wooden deck fittings

These tend to fall into the category which covers those fittings which need to be light but not necessarily that strong, such as masts, non-functioning items, solid objects which would be too heavy in brass, or complicated items which will require carving. As an example, the mast on *Coringa* was made from wood as a solid brass bar would have been too heavy and put excess weight high

above the centre of gravity. To make transportation easier the mast has a brass sheath at the bottom which fits into a brass tube, so allowing the mast to be removed.

Other wooden items on the model are the fiddley grating, made from strips of *miralite* plywood within an outer frame also from *miralite*. The quadrant grating is made from strips of 1.5mm (1⁄16in) plywood with hollow brass legs which fit over brass pins in the deck so allowing the grating to be removed if necessary. The ladders from the bridge house deck were made from *miralite* plywood but they may have been better in plastic card.

Plastic or Perspex deck fittings

Plastic card is often useful for objects

too small to be made from plywood which has a tendency to shatter when cut into thin strips for items such as ladders. Very thin plastic card, 0.3mm, can also be used to build clinker-style hulls for lifeboats. The only plastic card items on *Coringa* are the lifeboats and the body of the capstan mechanism. The capstan itself and the steam pistons were turned from brass.

Clinker lifeboats from plastic card

This is not the only way to build a lifeboat but it does produce one that is most impressive. The first stage is to make a wooden plug to the shape of the boat to be built (it can also be used as a dummy boat if required). When shaping the hull use a piece of card cut to the half transverse section shape at various points along the hull; this will help to keep the hull symmetrical by checking it against the card template.

When the plug is ready, cut strips of 0.3mm thick plastic card to form the hull planks. The width of these strips depends on the size of the boat. In theory all strips should be tapered at both ends on one edge only because of the difference in the half girth of the boat at mid-length and that at the stem and stern. The length round the edge (girth) from

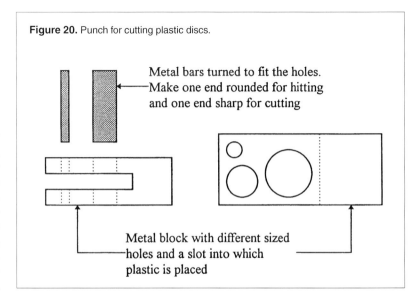

Figure 20. Punch for cutting plastic discs.

Metal bars turned to fit the holes. Make one end rounded for hitting and one end sharp for cutting

Metal block with different sized holes and a slot into which plastic is placed

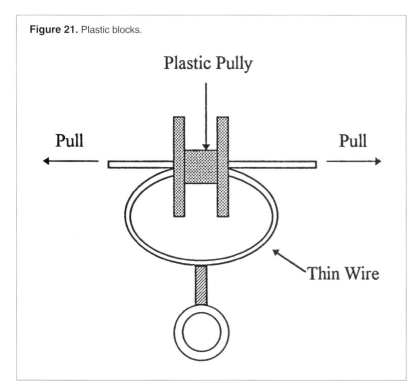

Figure 21. Plastic blocks.

Plastic Pully

Pull

Pull

Thin Wire

the top of boat to the keel must be divided into the same number of equally spaced marks at the bow, centre and stern. These marks can then be used to achieve evenly spaced planks, allowing for at least 2mm overlap on the planks.

Because of the difference between the girth of the plug amidships and that at stem and stern, each plank will have to be tapered to fit correctly on these reduced widths while still maintaining the required overlap.

If the boat has a flat transom cut this out of 1mm plastic card, secure to the plug with masking tape and sand flat with the plug. Begin construction by placing the first planks along the keel so that they form a V shape. Glue and hold at the stern first, and when dry repeat at the bow but crimp the plastic strips tightly with finger pressure so that a good joint is formed. When this is dry, glue the planks along the keel. Repeat the operation for all other planks, but first dry fit each piece to check that it lies correctly. To pre-

vent any planks sticking to the plug during the gluing process it should be thoroughly waxed before starting work. Photographs 18 to 22 show the various stages in lifeboat construction.

Perspex lifebuoys

Apart from the obvious use for thin Perspex sheet in windows, thick sheets and extrusions (sections) also come in useful as they are lighter than brass. Lifebuoys, for example, can be made from a Perspex rod or thick sheet. Regulation lifebuoys have an outside diameter of 30in (76cm) and an inside diameter of 18in (38cm) with an oval cross-section. At the time this tug was built they would have been of cork, canvas covered, with a grab line secured to it in four places by 4in wide canvas bands.

On a sheet of 2mm Perspex draw two concentric circles, one ⅜in diameter and one ⅝in diameter. After drilling the smaller hole, cut the Perspex to the shape of the larger circle, and sand the edges. Before sanding

the ring to the correct oval cross-section, divide it into four equal quarters and put a pencil mark on the outer edge at these points. Drill two small holes centrally on the edge of the ring, one either side of each mark. They must be large enough to accept the cord which will represent the grab lines. Thick cotton or Dacron cord can be used with a 0.7mm hole. A shallow groove must be made on the inside rim between each pair of holes to take the cord. It is advisable to paint the lifebuoys before threading the cord. Figure 19 shows the completed article.

The stowage racks for the lifebuoys were each made from three pieces of thin brass shim soft soldered into a Y shape with the ends bent over to hold the lifebuoy in place. For simplicity on the model a ½in rivet in the centre holds it to the superstructure.

Plastic blocks

Plastic card is ideal for making small blocks because it is easy to punch out small circular discs. A simple home-made punch is shown in Figure 20. The blocks on the lifeboat davits were made this way. Always cut the slot before the holes as the metal can distort due to internal stresses when the slot is cut. To make a block take two large discs and one small disc, of a size appropriate for the block to be made. Glue all three together, with the smaller disc in the centre, and drill a 1mm hole through the centre of all three discs. Take a piece of thin wire about 50mm long, twist the centre around a small diameter piece of brass to form an eye. Thread the loose ends through the block as shown in Figure 21. Pull the loose ends in opposite directions to tighten and trim off any excess wire. Thick cotton thread can be used for the rope in the tackles on the davits. Hooks can also be made in place of the eyes by cutting open an eye and bending to shape.

to be continued ❏

Owner's Delight

by J Pottinger

Readers of this journal will recall that in issue 98 Mr J H Barber described the building of his model of the Shetland double-ended boat *Owner's Delight*, illustrated with photographs of the various stages of construction, and a view of the boat as built.

Noting his excellent completed model in the Fishing Museum at Anstruther, Fife, some time ago I made a note to draw up a set of model plans showing the boat as built in 1911.

As he confirmed much of the past history of this boat I will not repeat it but will say that one of my former teachers at the Lerwick Central School in Shetland, Mr Tom Moncrieff, converted the former fishing boat into a seagoing cruising yacht in 1937, his plans of the conversion being published in an issue of the magazine *Yachting Monthly*.

The design follows the traditional Shetland double-ended clinker

View of the *Auk*, a boat I once owned on the Clyde in the 1970s. She was built in 1958 by Scalloway boatbuilder Jesse Goudie as the *Henrietta*, of larch on steamed oak frames. Her length was 21ft overall and beam 7ft, with Bermudan rig, and fitted with Stuart Turner 1.5bhp petrol engine; the drive was out of the starboard quarter. This engine was somewhat underpowered, and without reverse gear, thus ensuring that manoeuvring under sail to pick up a mooring had to be precise!

I discarded some inside ballast, and fitted compensating weight by adding steel plates on the outside of the keel.

Although smaller than the *Owner's Delight* the basic appearance is similar. Note the absolutely fair run of the planking, and generally fine lines.

In contrast is the later *Auk*, my brother's boat, 23ft long and nearly 8ft beam. She was built by Walter Duncan purely as a motor boat, and has a much beamier hull with fuller ends, but still has the sawn frames of the traditional construction.

A group of traditional Shetland boats. The boat in the centre, another by Walter Duncan, was built at the outset as a motor boat, and the slightly fuller bilge and stern can be noted in comparison with the two other purely sailing and rowing boats.

The laid up 45ft *Sylvanus*, which was built by Walter Duncan Snr in the early part of the twentieth century for partner owners which included my grandfather, and father later. She marked the transition from the purely sailing sixern to the larger powered fishing boats.

design, being a direct descendent of the Scandinavian longship design and construction, many of the features of construction being retained down to the present day, although sometimes modified and refined to suit current operating conditions and materials.

This boat was unique in that she was fitted with an auxiliary steam engine, which was soon replaced by a succession of more practical and efficient internal combustion engines. Nevertheless, she can claim to have been the first steam-propelled boat built in Shetland.

I have drawn the plans and rigging arrangement to represent the boat as built. It has been based on the one surviving photograph, and follows fairly conventional practice.

The foremast is stepped on the keel, and is held upright by a bar slotted in the mast box partners. The remainder of the open slot is sealed by a portable hatch cover. The mizzen mast is similarly stepped on top of the keel, and is supported up against the after end of the steering well. The main sheet leads to a horse fitted on top of the coaming, the jib sheets being hooked to suitably placed eyebolts on the foredeck. The small mizzen has its sheet block hooked on to a short bridle on the rudder head. The jib has its luff hanked on to the forestay, and the main has hoops around the mast, while the mizzen is set as a standing lug.

No internal details are included, and my drawings show the boat with the later raised bulwarks, but with the original low rail arrangement also included. The modeller can choose which arrangement to adopt.

The steering gear is a simple square-threaded rod and nut type, the rod being held captive in bearings supported by a tripod bracket. When the rod is turned by the steering wheel, the nut, which is connected directly by a curved yoke to the rudder, travels along the rod and moves the rudder in the required direction.

There is a deep well aft to take the helmsman. This has a hand pump in the forward corner, with the suction pipe leading down to the bottom of the boat.

Wrecked boat at Buckie of similar size to *Owner's Delight*. The arrangement of frames can be seen, those at the extreme ends, in local idiom are known as the stamrons, being somewhat similar to cant frames, not extending down to the keel. This boat had at one time been converted to a motor cruiser, the uncharacteristic flat deck beams, without camber, can be seen fitted on top of the carling running along the inside of the hull. When photographed she had been lying submerged for some time.

The vessel when sailing as the yacht *Veng*. This photograph was taken when she was lying at Kilcreggan on the Firth of Clyde in the early 1970s.   *Photographs by the author.*

The plans have been drawn at 1:24 scale, but they could well be enlarged to twice scale size to give a more substantial model, similar to that built by Mr Barber.

With rounded bilge these boats tended to heel quickly, then were very stable when sailing on the flatter plane of the bilge. My experience sailing my own similar boat confirmed that the initial stability seemed poor, but soon stiffened up when a certain angle of heel was reached.

In Shetland, clinker boats were always built with planks first then frames afterwards, temporary formers and braces being used to retain the hull shape until fully framed. This was determined largely by the shape of the planks themselves.

The frames were shaped and joggled to fit exactly over the plank landings, each frame being made up of a number of sections depending on the position in the boat.

The skill of the builders was often evidenced by the quality of the fit of the frame over the plank landings.

Each piece of the frames was cut with the grain as far as possible, and scarphed to its mating section. Traditionally the lower frame piece over the keel was never fitted tight on top of the keel or hog piece, but had an arched limber clear of the keel.

No separate hog piece was fitted, but instead a bevelled rebate was cut on each side at the top of the keel to take the lower edge of the garboard strake.

All the features of the construc-

tion followed traditional practice, meeting the needs of low cost, utility, and sound workmanship, which varied only in minor detail between the different builders.

The local boatbuilders in my home village of Hamnavoe, Walter and Philip Duncan, following in their father's footsteps, were well respected for their skill and workmanship.

Except in rare instances everything was done by eye, aided by some simple wooden patterns and templates of stem and sternpost, etc.

For a fuller description of the methods they used I can do no better than recommend The National Maritime Museum Monograph No. 57, *The Shetland Boat*, by Adrian G Ostler.   ❏

Building the Mayflower

~~~

by Lionel C Meeker

Hull showing lifts made of ½in veneered particle board.

Hull before planking.

[*Although we were unable to include the Baker plans, we have left in references to them, and to specific items on these plans, for the benefit of modellers who may have or later acquire a set. Ed*]

The *Mayflower* must have been a very large ship judging from all the people who claimed their ancestors came over in it. But, by today's standards this small galleon-type merchant ship – about the length of six parked cars, most probably would not have been allowed out of the harbor let alone cross the stormy Atlantic with 102 people aboard.

To build a complete and accurate model of this ship one would ideally need the full-size shipyard plans drawn up by naval architect William A Baker, and used to build the replica, *Mayflower II*, in 1956 at the Stuart Upham Shipyard, Brixham, Devon, England.

Mayflower (*Mayflower II*) is 106.5ft overall, with a breadth of 25ft, and depth of 12.6ft; the tonnage was 181 tons.

Very little is really known about the original sixteenth-century ship. Many researchers have delved into old records and documents, seeking to reconstruct a vessel of those early days, when no plans were used. In 1926 Drs R C Anderson, PhD and J W Horrocks were the first to find data with which to build a model or perhaps, later, a replica. Dr Anderson came up with a figure of 90ft from stem to sternpost; other than that, it is most likely Baker used the Anderson work to design and construct *Mayflower II*, thus enabling modellers to come as close to the original as possible. Anderson's model of 1926 now resides in the Hall of the Pilgrim Society, Plymouth, Massachusetts.

Other than what appears on Baker's plans for modellers, Kate Caffery, in her book, *The*

Mayflower, describes the living quarters of this ship. The so-called 'Great Cabin', in which the Mayflower Pact was signed, was about 15ft by 25ft, and on the main deck the space measured about 20ft by 75ft. A space of only about 18–20ft² was allotted to each person, according to Kate Caffery, less than the size of a standard bed!

Meals were cooked on an iron tray lined with sand called a firebox, situated under the forecastle deck, and conspicuously shown on the deck layout by a large rectangular chimney.

Even though *Mayflower* was considered a 'sweet clean ship', probably because of leakage from the wine cargoes seeping into the bilges and turning to vinegar, there were no facilities for sanitation and, as might be expected, sewage seeping into the hold created noisome odours. On the model, I added two 'seats of ease' sheltered by the beakhead bulkhead, accessible to the crew through the forward doors. This type of ship carried about 30 or 40 men.

Plans of *Mayflower II* are available from Plimoth Plantation in Plymouth, Massachusetts, USA for US $28.50 [*but this price should be checked. Ed*] William A Baker's plans include four 22in x 17in sheets showing profiles, sections, and waterlines, yards & miscellaneous details, masts, tops, crosstrees and a rigging profile. The plans are copyrighted and restrict the modeler to one model only. The plan scale is ⅛in = 1ft (1:96) except for the sheet of details at ¼in = 1ft scale (1:48). A few of the fittings unique to this type of vessel are shown in greater size and detail. Accompanying the plans are several pages of rigging instruction along with a separate painting schedule. Mr Baker in condensing his plans solely for the modeler, left out quite a bit of necessary detail. As I wanted to build the model to 1/48 scale I had the necessary sheets enlarged. During the early part of construction, a friend sent me the

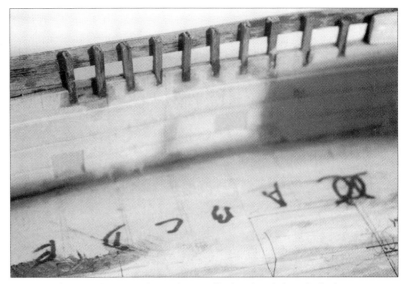

Simulated frame ends morticed into the top of bulwark and then planked over.

Gun deck bridged over by main deck beams. Note capstan and door and windows to Captain's cabin aft.

Hull planked with walnut strips. Masking tape still in place while bottom paint dries. 'Aged white' acrylic was the paint used.

plans for a Manila Galleon, the lines also by William A Baker but compiled and drawn up by Raymond Aker. Carolyn Freeman Travers, research manager for Plimoth Plantation, explained that Baker did not show enough detail with the *Mayflower* model plans as he was working on plans for a replica Spanish ship for the St Augustine Restoration Foundation shortly before his death. However, Mrs Travers and Peter Arenstam, Maritime Artisans Manager, kindly and quickly answered all the questions regarding technical features on *Mayflower II*.

Side by side, the Manila Galleon and *Mayflower* look remarkably similar. Disregarding the Spanish ship's unique decoration, the modeler can gain valuable insights into the structure of *Mayflower*. Most importantly it shows more clearly how *Mayflower's* bowsprit is offset to the right of the foremast then angles over to meet the centreline at the tip. The foretack bumpkins are also clearly detailed.

Most ship model articles begin with the usual descriptions of build-

Starboard bow detail.

ing the hull by the bread–and–butter method or a few other methods common to modelers. No matter what method, each has its peculiar problems, difficulties and challenges. *Mayflower* has more than its share.

Conveniently, Baker drew out his waterlines at 2ft spacing, each equal to ½in at 1:48 scale. On the body plan, each layer is marked from 0 at the baseline to the 40ft level at the top of the stern rail. Each level or 'lift' is equal to 2ft.

For the lifts, I used furniture grade particle board, each side covered with hardwood veneer. This particle board is in 4ft by 8ft sheets, and is expensive, but I was able to buy some left-overs from a local cabinet maker.

I laid out the waterlines that reach the 18ft level on thin white-painted aluminum sheet. On each, I scribed in the station lines. With the lines all clearly marked, I used a pair of scis-

sors to cut out each pattern then transferred each to a piece of the particle board. These were sawn to shape on the outside, and the centre of each was cut away to leave enough surface for glue. The stiff aluminum patterns make it easier to scribe in the half-breadth curves to the opposite sides of the boards.

The lifts above the 18ft level up to the top represent the ship's steep sides and tumblehome. I glued all the lifts together using the station lines as alignment guides. I worked the inboard sides down very thin as the frame structure is revealed along five different levels. Fine particle board has no grain and therefore is easy to grind down with rotary sanders.

Another important feature of the hull not shown on any of the plans, is the omission of one plank just above the upper wale at deck level so as to drain off water from the deck.

This can be seen on the replica of

the *Golden Hinde*, as can the small lead-lined scuppers, also present on *Mayflower II*.

I left the hull lifts solid up to level 12 because the deep draft waterline and lower deck level meet at the Dead Flat station. Above level 12, the upper lifts worked down quite thin and could break quite easily. They could be reinforced quickly with the transverse bulkheads.

From the aft stations (1 to 12), there are four different deck levels terraced along the length of the hull up to the steep sheer of the taffrail. Forward from station F to J, the forecastle structure is at one level only, and the frame ends are exposed about ½in below the rail. I used the extra photocopy patterns, applied to the hull, to mark the openings that the many sheer lines delineated by moldings, and ensure that they would be fair and parallel. Of course there are other ways to show the

Rigging started. The mainstay collar has been rove through a hole in the stem piece.

open hull structure, but I thought it easier to cut beveled segments of strip wood and insert each in place with tweezers. When firmly in place, I squirted superthin cyanoacrylate glue into the joints where I could not mortise the bottom pieces in place. Baker's plan C shows all the deck beams and carlins. Each beam has its own lodge knee. I put in a few token beams to outline the hatches and to furnish sufficient support for the deck above. Also shown is the deck planking width but omits the nibbing strakes at the deck ends. Such a feature may be taken for granted and put on a model if the deck is plainly visible to viewers.

I made the decks by first fitting a cardboard pattern into the hull making sure it fitted snugly to the bulwarks, and that the centreline matched the hull centreline. For the deck planks, ⅛in wide, I ripped about 75 strips from clear birch tongue depressors. I have found this material more convenient than milling long strips from raw lumber. I rubbed one edge of each plank with a china marking pencil, squared off the ends and glued each to the cardboard pattern starting at the centreline. If the deck is very long, I sight along the pattern as the first couple of strakes are being fitted to make sure there are no 'wavy' spots along the edges. The Rules of Planking probably have not changed much in hundreds of years, except perhaps how each plank is fastened to the beams. Wolfram zu Monfeld, in his book, *Historic Ship Models*, shows a diagram of the so-called 'shift of butts' or the usual mode of planking to ensure butts are not too close together. A little care and preplanning will result in a professional looking deck, noting of course, that the fastenings are over beams. I placed imitation treenails on the decks. Over the years, on a real ship, these pegs get bleached out and are hardly visible.

Another detail not on the plan is the thickness of the gun port lids. Again Mr Arenstam of Plimoth Plantation came to the rescue and advised me that the lids are twice the thickness of the hull planking around the gunports. In this case the planking here was 2in thick.

Mayflower mounted at least three types of cannon. The largest of these were the Sakers, 10ft long with a 4in bore; the other large piece was the Minion, 7ft 6in long with a 3½in bore. It is hoped that the Pligrims had all this armament stowed below as there was hardly enough living space below decks besides having the risk of a loose cannon during heavy weather. Baker's plans showed no guns so I did not put any on the model.

Among *Mayflower's* deck levels, the main deck runs all the way from the forecastle bulkhead to the aft transom. Below this, the gun deck runs from stem to stern. Above the main deck is the long quarterdeck with a surprising overhead clearance of 6ft. This space is divided by two bulkheads, the foremost being the capstan room, aft of this is the space allotted to the helmsman who handles the whipstaff, a long pole swiveled on to the tiller just beneath the deck. The quarterdeck terminates aft in the Great Cabin, is about 11ft long and a little over 10ft wide. Over the Great Cabin is the captain's quarters, even smaller, and decked over to form what I would call 'the upper quarterdeck'. Plan B shows the necessary athwartships sections with the bulkhead planking, ladders, doors and windows. The entrances to the forecastle and the cabin decks aft are known as 'Cubbridge Heads', an archaic term I found only in the Oxford English Dictionary. The horizontal planking of the bulkheads is not shown in detail but may be inferred as 'overlapping'. I left the aft Cubbridge Head open but marked by a set of hanging knees fitted to turned support posts. Other bulkheads were made solid.

With the interior completed I

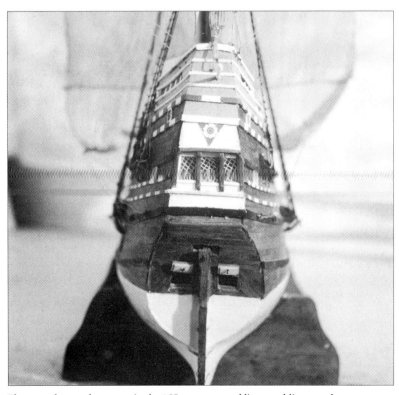

Photographs can show up mistakes! Here two out-of-line mouldings can be seen.

Port side forward. The anchor has been secured for sea along the forward channel.

decided to plank the hull with strips of walnut finishing them with two coats of Danish Oil Finish rather than using buff as noted on the painting schedule. The hull planking went on very easily and I did not have to steam or force any around the curves. Finally, using a Starrett machinist's height gauge I marked off the load waterline with masking tape and painted the bottom with an off-white model water-based paint. I also used the Danish Oil Finish around the upperworks to give the impression of a sea worn merchant-man rather than the gaudy look often seen on kit models. I used flat dark red autobody primer on the head rails, but used a gold pen to scribe in the trailboard ornaments.

I put buff paint on the insides of the gun ports, which I left open with the lids raised and secured.

Another large opening in the hull is the rectangular one for the rudder stock, show on plan B (stern eleva-tion). At sea, in rough weather, *Mayflower II* did not have leakage here as the tiller opening is fitted with a large canvas boot.

Windows are fitted to the stern and sides. There are three stern win-dows in a horizontal line; the middle one is double and opens inward. To simulate the old-fashioned diamond shaped panes, I mounted the window frames on to plastic sheet then strung ⅟₆₄in white draughtsman tape diagonally across both sides and nipped the ends with a razorblade. The completed windows fitted neatly into their pre-cut openings.

In addition to the painting sched-ule, attention is called to Station 9 on plan B. This half-section shows the colours of all the moulding strips (7) and the planking in between. Three of the wide mouldings are striped in 'Earth Green' and 'Oyster White'. The 'green' is not defined so

I used a basic hue and some off-white and prepainted these mould-ings in alternate half-inch segments. I did not attempt any more trim other than the white outlines of the win-dows and the short upper mould-ings. The green and white strips forming guard rails nicely comple-mented the stained, hand-rubbed walnut planking. I omitted the other colours as too garish for a hard-working merchantman. In spite of the research for *Mayflower II*, I am of the opinion that the Pilgrims char-tered an old almost worn out craft and any available money would have been better spent on rope and sails, not expensive paint.

While Raymond Aker's Manila Galleon plans furnish much of the detail for Baker's small scale *Mayflower* plan, the photos I took of the replica *Golden Hinde* provided a good insight into how these old ships were probably built.

Foremast ramshead block is abaft the foremast. The galley stack lid is in the foreground.

In spite of needed detail on Baker's plans, his rigging profile is easy to follow. Better yet, Baker lists exact rope sizes and the larger scale drawings show the topsail yard parrels and deadeyes in proper detail. Another sheet shows the size and shape of the unique ramshead blocks and the shapes of seventeenth-century common blocks salvaged from Kalmar Harbour, Sweden.

Mayflower's rigging was all done using the time-honored arts of the seaman and the shipwright. The three masts are joined to topmasts in the traditional manner except for the round finely structured mast tables,

Starboard quarter. Much of the painted decoration was purposely omitted.

which may prove to be a challenge to the model builder. I elected to make mine from cut-down craft shop wooden flower pots, working these to size, then gluing in the internal and external battens.

Mayflower carried six sails only, not counting the bonnets laced to the courses, the lateen and spritsail. There are no jibs or staysails.

Rather than using silkspan paper for the sails, I thought some threadbare old polyester white cloth would look more convincing. I dyed the stuff in strong tea and judiciously applied cyano glue around the edges of the boltropes and cringles to give a real sea-stained look to the probable old worn sails of the original ship.

Another unique feature of these old ships is the so-called 'Martnets' –

spidery brail-like lines rigged with deadeyes and blocks as an aid to furling the large square sails and lateen. In those early days footropes beneath the yards were not used. In place of reefing, the lower sails divided by about a third with a bonnet, were lowered to the deck, the bonnet unlaced and quickly removed. To furl the sail, the billowing top section was gathered in using the martnets.

I omitted martnets on the model because I could not get them to hang properly as shown on the plan. The mainsail has four sets of these that overlap the usual set of the bowline bridles.

The topgallant masts fly two flags. The Cross of St George on the fore and the Union Flag minus the Cross of St Patrick on the main. I

made the flags from silkspan paper, using painted superthin Micropore surgical tape glued over the silkspan for the crosses. Silkspan is almost transparent and it is easy to match both sides of the flag with the stuck-on segments.

Mayflower's yards are completely drawn out on Plan B and show all the necessary details, including the rigging stops on the yardarms. To make these stops I clamped short square lengths of wood to the yards, sealed them firmly with glue, then drilled the tops for a treenail just to make sure. I could then trim and shape the stops to their optimum size without fear of collapse.

For treenails I found the stiff natural dark brown fibres from a worn-out deck scrubber were ideal. The fact that all these fibres are not the

Main top.

Mainstay, showing the enormous five-hole deadeye set up.

same diameter makes them even more convenient when I secure larger planks or beams.

Plan C shows the details of the masts, partners, and crosstrees. The mast doublings show the usual hole with a square one directly beneath. I drilled the round hole and fudged the square one by sawing out an exact rectangle through the edge, then inserting a filling piece in the open end to form the square hole. It is also easier to make three or four of these at a time, slicing them up as needed. A hardwood such as maple is ideal for this job.

I made the large mast stays from leftover cable-laid nylon fish line, serving the parts with black thread where the stays pass round the mast and to enclose the large deadeyes used when setting up the stays.

As one of the plans shows, ovoid deadeyes support the shrouds. Fortunately commercial model suppliers

stock these items to the right scale. Beneath the channels, also known as chain wales, the deadeyes are fastened to the hull by what appear to be long-link chain. On *Mayflower*, the outboard edge of the fore channel is parallel to the curve of the hull. There are no mizzen channels.

Forward of the fore channels, the catheads arch out of the forecastle hull planking. Each cathead is fitted with two sheaves for the anchor handling tackle.

Though *Mayflower* was not a Royal Navy ship, many of the shipboard practices were common to seamen everywhere. Neither *Mayflower* nor the Manila Galleon plans show how the anchors were fished and catted. For this procedure I refer the modeller to page 129 of the *Masting and Rigging of English Ships of War* by James Lees. This shows a diagram on how anchors were lifted and secured.

As I worked on the model, Mrs Travers and Peter Arenstam graciously answered all the technical questions regarding this ship as they came up.

For instance, the forward and main knightsheads, on which the ramshead purchases are rove, have an extra sheave. This fourth sheave acts as a fairlead for other lines when they are led to the capstan. The cargo tackle seized to the mainstay has its hauling part here.

I asked about the absence of bitt pins through the knightshead shafts. I was told that pins were not necessary as three or four turns of the halyard around the upper part of the knighthead held well enough. The hauling part, however, leads through the third sheave on the port side then to the capstan.

There is an apparent contradiction in the painting notes. Item 2 states 'main hull above waterline to

Stern view of completed model.

Photographs by the author.

be buff,' however the replica, in the fashion of most other ships of this period, carries the white bottom paint to the underside of the main wale.

The hull profile does not show a bolster around the hawse openings. On the model I put on a grooved hardwood extension beneath the hawse to ease the chafe on the cables. A photo of *Mayflower II* at sea shows a black bolster that completely surrounds the hawse hole.

I was also informed that the inboard bulwarks were not planked. The frame ends are rounded over and have a wale attached to the top outboard. This important feature is not shown on Baker's plan but shows on Ray Aker's Manila Galleon. There are no caprails, but I used them on the structures fore and aft of the main deck because I thought they looked better.

On *Mayflower*'s Plan D, (Rigging Details) a gammoning slot is shown but no gammoning around the bowsprit. The Manila Galleon shows one set of gammoning with six turns. Obviously there are two sets of gammon lashings on *Mayflower II* as I have been told, 'There are six turns on each of the gammon lashings.'

None of the plans for these old ships shows anchor linings beneath the catheads to protect the hull from damage while the anchors are heaved home.

Mayflower's cables are 12in in circumference and I used cable-laid rope a little less than 5⁄32in in diameter and bent them to puddened anchor rings with a round turn and two half-hitches. An alternate way would be to use the 'inside clinch.'

At this point it may be proper to comment about the ship's boats. There have been many references to the so-called shallop, or a lug-rigged two-masted fishing boat, for use in shallow waters – an obsolete craft.

This boat, with a capacity for 32 people, was said to have been partially dismantled and kept below decks. It did furnish sleeping space for some of the people. Since the shallop was not shown on any of the plans no more detailed comment is needed.

In contrast, *Mayflower*'s boat, stowed on deck, is meticulously drawn out on a separate sheet. The lines (buttocks and waterplanes) readily assist the modelmaker to construct an accurate hull. The second part of the plan shows the internal framing, the floor boards, thwarts, with thole pins and backing pieces. The rudder is not shown but an additional post forward of the sternpost, may have been used for a steering oar rowlock. There is a thwart to hold one mast forward; possibly a standing lug rig. The boat's top planks are clinker built while those from the keel outboard are carvel built. It must have been a jolly looking boat with a 7.5ft width or almost a third of its length of 24ft.

On the model I elected to keep the boat upright on skids, thereby making it easier for the crew to hook into the lifting bridle and launch the boat with the cargo tackle on the mainstay.

Rather than rig a boat cover, I left the interior open to scrutiny by adding a complement of oars, mast and sail, water cask and a bailing bucket. I omitted the bridle but fitted ringbolts fore and aft as would be required.

There is no mention of the painting scheme for this boat, and other modelers have merely used exclusively black or dark brown. On the model, the boat is lashed to the skids by hooks over the gunwales leading to ringbolts beneath and set up with several turns of rope. The skids are loose so the boat may be lifted out to inspect the details and hatchways on the main deck. ❏

Ketch *Irene*

by Albert Price

When built, *Irene* was a fine example of a typical West Country coasting ketch of her times. She was constructed in Bridgwater, Somerset, in 1907 by the well-known shipbuilder of Bridgwater F J Carver and Sons. She was owned locally by Messrs Clifford J Symonds and Clifford Symonds, and Captain William Lee (her future master). It was intended to operate her in the local trade to and from Bridgwater.

She measured 118ft from stern to tip of bowsprit, with a waterline of 83ft and beam of 21ft. From water level to button top on mainmast she had an overall height of 90ft.

The total sail area was 4687ft². The individual sail areas, in square feet were: main sail 1098, main top-sail 470, mizzen sail 782, mizzen topsail 270, stay sail 430, standing jib 308, boom 240, flying jib 286, square sail 803.

The hull was constructed of 3in thick Columbian Pine, double planking on English Oak frames with iron knees.

In 1966 Dr Leslie Morrish found *Irene* lying in the River Hamble in a

Three photographs of the completed 1/72 scale model of the ketch *Irene*.

Photographs by the author.

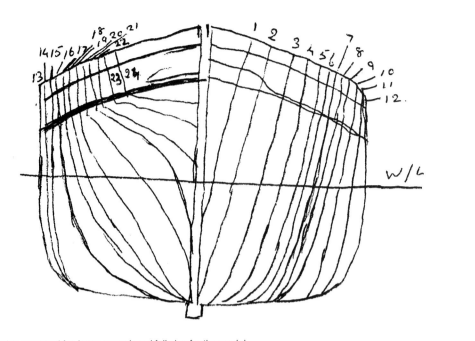

Figure 1. Body plan prepared for *Irene*, reproduced full size for the model.

derelict condition. He purchased her, and she was brought round to the Thames in London, where she was repaired and restored. The story of her discovery and restoration is told by Dr Morrish in his book *Good Night Irene*.

The model

The scale of the model is 1:72. I built the hull of the model on the egg-box method. I cut a longitudinal centre member from ³⁄₁₆in plywood which had the profile of the hull from keel to deck, and included the shape of stem and stern. I cut slots in this, from keel to waterline, at the positions where the frames (or in this case the solid formers) would be fitted. The set of plans which I had obtained did not include a body plan. After searching through my books I came across one which, with a few minor adjustments, met my requirements. The result is shown in Figure 1. I had decided to fit only each alternate frame (former), and these I cut to shape in ¼in ply from data from this body

plan. A slot was cut in each one from deck to waterline, and they were fitted and secured to the longitudinal member.

Blocks of wood were glued on each side of the longitudinal member from the foremost frame to the stem, and shaped for the bows. These would provide an anchorage for the planks. A similar arrangement was carried out at the stern abaft the aftermost frame.

The planks cut for the hull, and also those for the deck, were cut from wood ¹⁄₁₆in thick and made ⅛in wide.

The planks were glued and also held with dowels. These were made from split bamboo (cane). Holes ¹⁄₃₂in diameter were drilled and dowels inserted, glued, lightly tapped in, and cut off flush.

When planks needed to be bent to suit the shape of the hull, I soaked the part to be bent in boiling water and left it there overnight. I bent the plank between finger and thumb and put it in a jig to dry out.

Deckhouses and deck fittings

were made from wood, and painted light grey.

The masts and spars were made from dowels and shaped as needed. A narrow strip of paper ⅛in wide was glued round the mainmast ½in up from the deck. This was painted black, and six ¼in pins were inserted around to provide belaying points for the rigging. The same was done for the mizzenmast but only four pins were put in. Figure 2 is a diagram, not to scale, showing the various belaying points for the rigging.

The standing rigging was black thread and all other rigging was brown cotton. Blocks and deadeyes were made from ³⁄₁₆in dowel drilled and shaped.

When the deadeyes were joined in pairs I put three strands of cotton through the holes to represent the lanyards.

Rigging

The shrouds (thread) were looped over the top of the mast and made fast to the deadeye. The starboard forward one went on first, and then port, working alternately, making sure that the mast was not pulled out of alignment.

The ratlines were tied individually and given a dab of glue to hold them.

The sails were made of white paper, and curved by drawing it several times under a ruler.

Colour scheme

Lower hull to waterline: red.
Above waterline: light grey.
Deckhouses, deck fittings: grey.
Mast, bowsprit: natural wood, oiled. Stain.
Deck: red lead.
Inside bulwarks: light blue.
The dimensions of the model were: length overall 1ft 8in, height overall 1ft 4½in, width at widest point 3½in.

References

A set of plans of *Irene* can be obtained from: The Blake Museum, Blake Street, Bridgwater, Somerset TA6 3NB. Contact the museum for current prices.
Good Night Irene by Dr Leslie Morrish, published in 1985 by The February Press Ltd, Windsor, Berks.   ❏

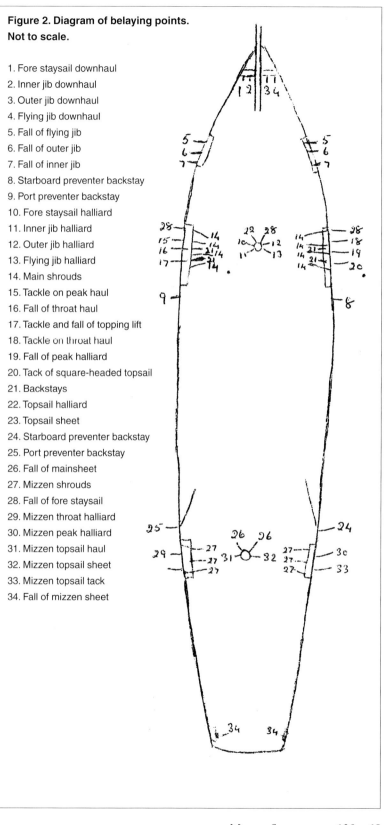

Figure 2. Diagram of belaying points. Not to scale.

1. Fore staysail downhaul
2. Inner jib downhaul
3. Outer jib downhaul
4. Flying jib downhaul
5. Fall of flying jib
6. Fall of outer jib
7. Fall of inner jib
8. Starboard preventer backstay
9. Port preventer backstay
10. Fore staysail halliard
11. Inner jib halliard
12. Outer jib halliard
13. Flying jib halliard
14. Main shrouds
15. Tackle on peak haul
16. Fall of throat haul
17. Tackle and fall of topping lift
18. Tackle on throat haul
19. Fall of peak halliard
20. Tack of square-headed topsail
21. Backstays
22. Topsail halliard
23. Topsail sheet
24. Starboard preventer backstay
25. Port preventer backstay
26. Fall of mainsheet
27. Mizzen shrouds
28. Fall of fore staysail
29. Mizzen throat halliard
30. Mizzen peak halliard
31. Mizzen topsail haul
32. Mizzen topsail sheet
33. Mizzen topsail tack
34. Fall of mizzen sheet

The LONDON MODEL ENGINEERING EXHIBITION 2003

7th GREAT YEAR

24th, 25th & 26th JANUARY 2003

at

WEMBLEY EXHIBITION CENTRE

MODEL ENGINEERING

FREE CAR PARKING

WORKING MODELS

Locomotives, Traction and Stationary Engines, Workshop Tools, etc.
– *PLUS* –
ALL THE LEADING SPECIALIST SUPPLIERS

LIVE STEAM Locomotives and *HOT AIR ENGINES* IN ACTION

The South's leading Model Engineering Exhibition!

MARINE MODELLING
See all types of boats from the man of war to modern tugs, yachts, etc.

Superb displays by leading model engineering clubs & societies

OPEN 10.30am until 6.00pm Friday & Saturday, 10.30am until 5.00pm Sunday
(Last Admissions 4.00pm)

ADMISSION: ADULT £8 SENIOR £7 CHILD £5 FAMILY (2 Adults + 3 Children) £21
SAVE £££'s BY BOOKING IN ADVANCE – TELEPHONE THE TICKETLINE 01926 614101

Organised by Meridienne Exhibitions Ltd, The Fosse, Fosse Way, Leamington Spa, Warks. CV31 1XN

© Meridienne Exhibitions Ltd. 2002

An Aid to Seizing Blocks

by H Picard

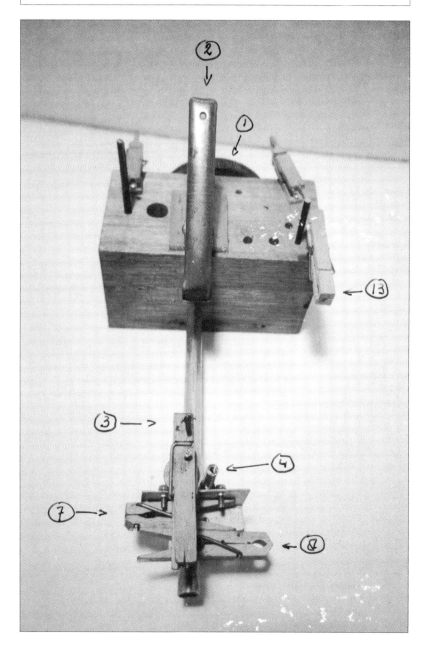

Photograph 0 and 1. The basis of this tool is a rectangular block of smooth hardwood about 8cm square and 15cm long. The back of this block is fitted with a metal support piece 1. A simple spring clamp 2 is secured to the top of the wood block. The jaws of this clamp should shut closely and evenly. This can be achieved by drawing a smooth flat file through the closed clamp.

A piece of metal tube about 25cm long is fixed in the middle of the front, about 3cm from the bottom. A piece of metal with a hole is fitted tight round this tube, is then placed on it. A screw is fitted on the bottom, to fasten this piece of metal on each desired spot of the tube. A little metal plate is fixed on the top of this piece of metal, so a clothes peg can be fixed on the top of this plate. This clothes peg is situated on the same level as clamp 2.

At about 15mm distance a nut or something similar is fixed, to allow a second clothes peg 5 or 6 to be put there. This clothes peg is secured by a screwbolt 4 and can be moved horizontally.

Two clothes pegs 7 and 8 are placed in the horizontal position against the back of the metal plate, under the clothes pegs 3 and 5. Clothes peg 7 is fastened to the plate and clothes peg 8 is fixed to number 7 in the opposite way. At the right end of the wooden block, left for left-handed people, I have fixed a clothes peg 13 in such a way that the jaws are at the same level as the jaws of clamp 2. This clothes peg 13 is used to stabilize tool 12.

Photograph 7. The clothes pegs are all of wood and their form is altered according to my idea. The mouth is smoothed with a piece of sandpaper, to make them close perfectly. The front is shortened and bevelled.

Clothes peg 3. I drilled a 0.5mm hole through both jaws from top to bottom. The hole in the lower jaw is enlarged to 0.8mm. In the upper

0. Side view of the completed tool.

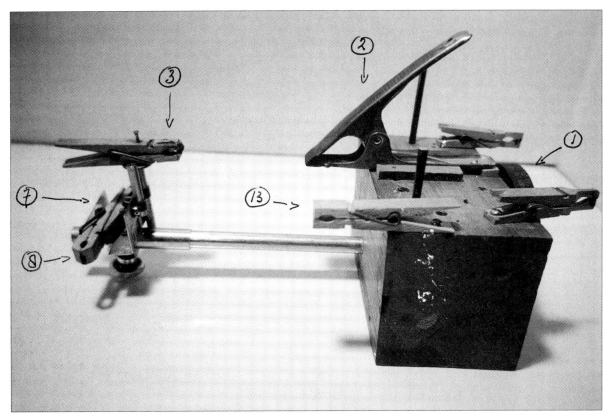

1. Front view of the completed tool.

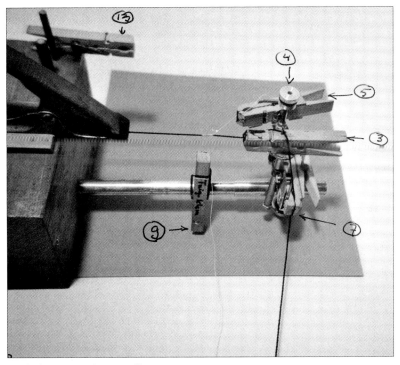

2. The beginning of an eyesplice.

hole a peg is placed projecting about 3mm into the lower hole. The protruding part at the top is cut off and smoothed. On the right side for left-handed people, or on the left side for right-handed people a peg is placed of which the head protrudes about 2mm. A peg or nail with the head protruding about 3mm is fastened on the middle of the top of this clothes peg. Clothes peg 5: this is of the same type but the two pegs with their protruding heads are omitted. Clothes peg 6: this is as number 5, but the jaws are made very narrow, about 3-4mm. Pegs 7 and 8, 9 and 13: they have the same form as No. 3, but all the peg additions are left off.

I also use a small hook 11, made from a paper clip fixed on a wooden stick. This has two small flat levels and the part behind this level is of sufficient length that when this stick is fixed in clamp 2, the tail of the stick lies under the spring of clamp 2. So the hook is secure and at the

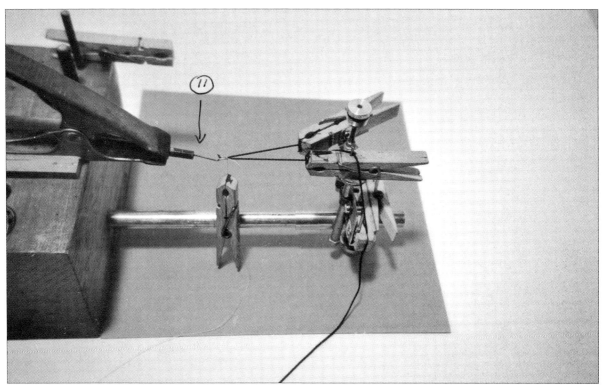

3. Half way through making the eyesplice.

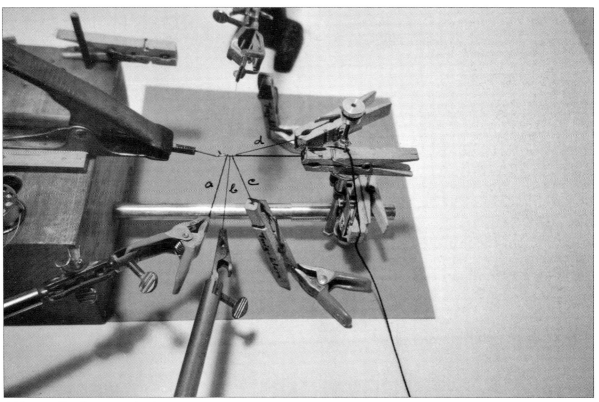

4. The eyesplice almost completed.

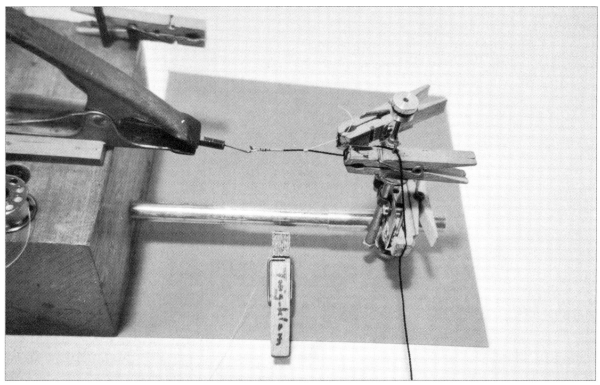

5. The eyesplice completed and a start made on a mouse.

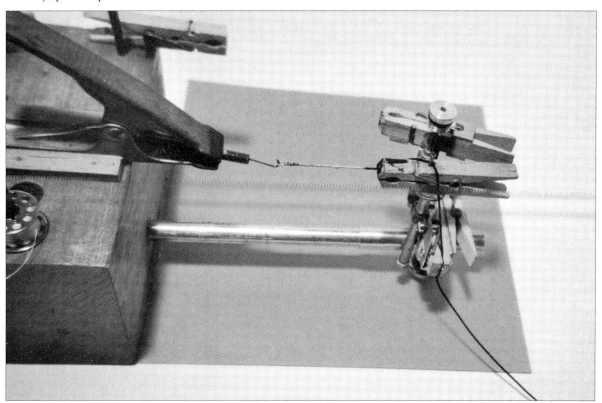

6. The completed mouse.

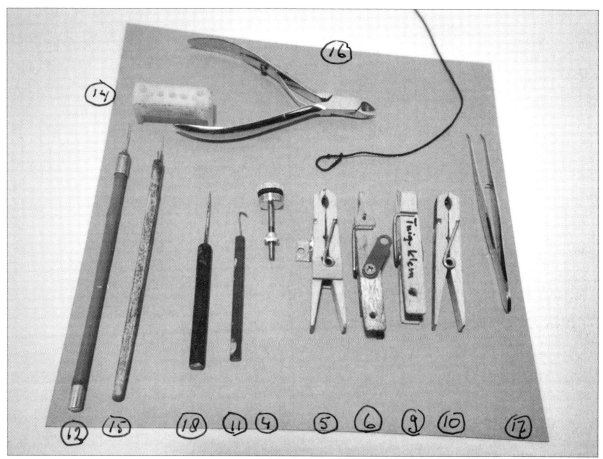

7. All the tools used.

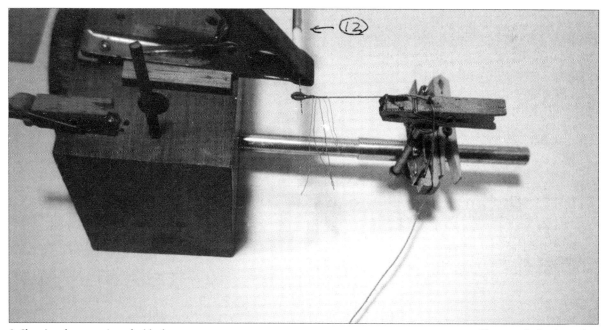

8. Showing the stropping of a block.

Photographs by the author.

same level as clothes peg 3. I use a small pin 12 a little pointed dental drill mounted on a wooden stick. This stick has a diameter of 8mm, which makes it fit transversely in clothes peg 13. So I can fix peg 12 with a rigging block on it in a horizontal position in clamp 2 and clothes peg 13.

The serving aid in use

Photograph 2. I make an eye-splice in the following way. A rigging line of three to four strands is stretched between clamp 2 and clothes peg 3. Then the seizing line is secured by a clove hitch. The short end of the seizing line is secured in clothes peg 5, so that the knot does not rotate when winding the seizing line. It is also possible to secure with cyanoacrylate, but use very little of this glue. Then I start to wind the seizing line.

The seizing line should be made long enough to seize the eyesplice without interruption if possible. Now it can be seen why I put a piece of iron on the back of the tool. I place the tool on the edge of the table so the metal tube and also the rigging line are clear of the table, and I have space to move my hands. Should I knock against the tool by accident it will not move, thus avoiding damage during the rigging process. When the tool is fixed directly to the table and it is knocked, possibly some damage could be done to the work in progress.

Photograph 3. After winding on some turns, I fasten the seizing line with a stitch, take the rigging line out of the tool, place the hook 11 and fold the seized part of the rigging line around the hook. The shortest end is fixed in clothes peg 5 and the longest end in clothes peg 3. I secure the eye with a clove hitch of the seizing line, put on a little bit of cyanoacrylate and wind on several turns. Then I release the short part of the rigging line from clothes peg 5 and untie the 3–4 strands. Now I start again with winding, but one

Figure 1. Showing alterations to standard wood clothes pegs.

STANDARD WOOD CLOTHES PEG

PEG No 3

PEG No 5

HOLE FOR SCREW No 4

HOLE FOR SCREW No 4

PEG No 6

TURNED 90 DEGREESS RELATIVE TO PEG No 5

strand remains outside the seizing, after four windings the second strand is kept outside the seizing and so on.

Photograph 4. When at last all the strands are outside and the seizing is also finished and secured with a little cyanoacrylate, I cut the protruding strands. It is important to do this as evenly as possible. Therefore do not use a pair of scissors but a pair of nippers 16. When done in the correct way, a perfect eye seizing or block seizing will be obtained. There are many more types of small seizings. which can be done in the tool.

On photographs 5, 6 and 7 an eyesplice and a mouse can be seen on a headstay I made for 1:96 scale, 3m long galliot of 1760. Photograph 8 shows some examples of seized blocks.   ❏